Published by Hellgate Press
(An imprint of L&R Publishing, LLC)

Hellgate Press
PO Box 3531
Ashland, OR 97520
www.hellgatepress.com
email: sales@hellgatepress.com

Editor: Harley B. Patrick
Interior design: Michael Campbell, MCWriting.com
Cover design: L. Redding

ISBN: 978-1-55571-7506

Library of Congress Cataloging-in-Publication Data
Madsen, Angela.
Rowing against the wind / Angela Madsen. -- First edition.
pages cm
1. Madsen, Angela. 2. Women rowers--United States--Biography. 3. Rowers--United States--Biography. 4. Athletes with disabilities--United States--Biography. 5. Veterans--United States--Biography. 6. Self-realization--United States. I. Title.
GV790.92.M337A3 2013
797.12'3092--dc23
[B]
2013049120

Printed and bound in the United States of America
First edition 10 9 8 7 6 5 4 3 2 1

When I pray, I pray for strength… to be able!

To be able to endure pain and suffering

To be able to overcome challenges and obstacles

To be able to stay focused on my goals

To be able to do the work

I pray for the strength to do what I need to do on my own,

not for a miracle or for someone to do it for me.

This is my life.

I am not waiting for it to change.

I am not waiting for the world to change;

I am changing what I can.

Vita mutatur, non tollitur: Life is changed, not taken away.

ROWING AGAINST THE WIND

—

ANGELA MADSEN

CONTENTS

ACKNOWLEDGMENTS

Thanks to the rest of the world's most unlikely rowers and to my wife, Debra Moeller, who has gone "all in" in support of all of my projects. No one does it alone and I contribute a lot of my success to Debs, as she is known to ocean rowers in the UK. Franck Festor and I would not have made it to the starting line of the Atlantic Rowing Race 2007 without her help.

Thanks go out to everyone who did an article or interview and to everyone who forwarded an e-mail and said, "Check this out."

For all of my friends on Facebook, Twitter and the World Rowing Network, I am appreciative and grateful.

Huge thanks to all of the naysayers and people who went out of their way to make it more difficult because without all of you it would just feel too easy!

Also to my three granddaughters, and everyone really: remember that no matter how bad things get you are not totally powerless, you always have choices. Situation and circumstance should never be allowed to oppress you and dictate who you are and what you are able to achieve in your lifetime. I want you to be happy and successful, to dream big and set higher goals for yourselves and to always realize the possibilities and potential for success. Always be hopeful and willing to do what is necessary to achieve whatever goals you set for yourselves.

I want to thank everyone for their support and for liking the dedicated Facebook pages "Military & Veteran Tribute Row" and "Angela Madsen."

I would also like to express my thanks and appreciation to the following: Abilities Expo, Star Cushion, Swiftwick, Rock Tape, Shared Adventures, Perky Jerky, West Marine Long Beach store #00012, Team Kehei, Action Advocates, Paralympic Sport Clubs (Menlo Park, Sacramento, Santa Cruz and Silicone Valley), AccessSurf Hawaii, Equality TV, Orlando

Rogers Foundation, Paralyzed Veterans of America--California Chapter, Disabled Dealer, Ranita Marcellino-Ruddle, Jo Ann Pine, Robert Soto, Grandee R, Elizabeth Oakley, Bobby Vittore, Jill Nakano, Kellie Wheeler, Tina Musto, Peggy Strople, Mary Morton, Delores Pereira, Margo Mott , Maureen Lyons, Ann Desalernos, Steve Baloff , Denise Louie, John Bull, Heidi Black, Scott Neuse, Josephine Alvarez, Steven Grove, Mark Stuessy, Courtney Casey, Bret Davies, Beverly Hopkins, MaryKatherine Kuner, Vivian Snyder, Sharon Kelleher, Mary Shuttleworth, Mr Warren Lund and Janice B. Edwards.

Many thanks as well for the safe return of *Spirit of Orlando* go out to H&M Landing, Catherine Miller, the crew of *Old Glory* and owner/operator Joe Philiips, Bobby Turner, Alex Centner, Richard McDonald, John Chustine, Tory Shane DeNuccio, Ray Kommel of Bakersfield, Lott Mason of San Clemente, Roy Rafferty of San Clemente, Ted Lizge of Laguna Nigel, Troy Regan of Dana Point, Brian Wilson of San Clemente, Juan Contreras of San Diego, Luis Godinaz of Chula Vista, Alfred Orozco of Southgate, John Nix of Garden Grove, Kathleen Barcelona of Garden Grove, James Willis of Capistrano Beach, Mike Hatzidakis of Colton, Trent J Levinson of Desert Hot Springs, Richard Allen of San Diego, Glen Lee Borgia of San Clemente, Gaetono Legrande of Dana Point, Todd Lake of San Juan, Daniel Craig of San Clemente, Chad Psilopoulos of Oceanside and Brian Muecke of Rim Forest.

Thank you all so much,
Angela & your *Old Glory* catch of the day, *Spirit Of Orlando*

"There can be no really pervasive system of oppression without the consent of the oppressed."

— FLORENCE R. KENNEDY

"Nobody can make you feel inferior without your consent."

— ELEANOR ROOSEVELT

INTRODUCTION

I did not choose this life; this life was chosen for me.

No one chooses to be disabled or to endure a life of pain and suffering. But like everyone else on the planet, disabled or not, we have a choice to either live and walk in truth…or not. The famous jazz singer Pearl Bailey once said, "You never find yourself until you face the truth." I've had to face my share of truths more than once in my life.

As I collected my thoughts and memories to write this book, I wished that I had spent more time walking in the truth. No matter how hard or easy it was to pull those thoughts and feelings together – some tragic, some victorious – I had to stay on the path of truth. You'll find the pages in this book to be filled with honesty – there is no sugar coating, no wistful wishing, just the honest truth.

For most of my life, I did not allow myself to believe that things really do happen for a reason. It is my experience that our life's purpose may or may not be revealed at a later time. From time to time, I get bits and pieces that keep me on the correct path. I've come to realize that I may never get to see the big picture or realize my true purpose.

I do know that whatever my purpose is in this life, my differently-abled, physically-challenged, broken-down, beaten-up body seems to be the vehicle required for me to achieve it. When I go to church and the healers come upon me, I politely ask them to go away. I think it's funny that they don't seem to understand. It's not because I like pain and suffering, and it's not because I don't have faith, but rather, it's because I do have faith that I choose not to seek their services. Don't they get it? I am a spiritual person and I am this way for a reason. I am purpose-driven; I may suffer pain and not walk upright in this life, but when I go home, I will not suffer the walk through the gate. I can live with that. If I could go back and change things,

I would not. It would be nice not to have to suffer so much pain but, hey, that's just the way it is.

I am blessed to have the abilities that I have and I am doing exactly what I am supposed to be doing with those abilities. In the beginning, I was angry but now I completely understand. Everything really does happen for a reason. I am doing exactly what it is that I am supposed to be doing and I have to be this way in order to do it!

In sports like diving, skating, and snow boarding, the higher degree of difficulty, the greater the score. And I've scored pretty high. Living with a spinal cord injury could be considered a major difficulty, but the goals I've set and reached are phenomenal. And I'm proud and honored to say that achievements such as mine are shared by only a few and are revered and celebrated by even the most physically capable non-disabled athletes in the world.

PREFACE

According to the Census Bureau, 51.2 million Americans have some level of disability; that's 18% of the population.

But those are just numbers on a page. When the disabled person is also a veteran there is an added disadvantage. People seem to be under the impression that our government takes care of all of the needs of veterans and that we are given everything. At times I didn't want to admit I was a veteran, especially in the disabled community.

I hold no animosity or ill will towards any of the doctors, students or nurses who were responsible for my care or lack there of at the Veterans Hospital. I was recently asked, "If you could be face to face with the people responsible for your current medical condition, what would you do?" Believe it or not, my answer's always the same, "Forgive them." And I have, in fact, forgiven them. The public knows very little about the medical care we receive as veterans or that our medical centers are teaching hospitals. It is the system of benefits adjudication and claims that separates them from other teaching hospitals. I hope that my experiences as I described in these pages will shed some much-needed light on what goes on in these places and how veterans are treated.

I am sure the medical students, interns and nurses who were following orders may also have suffered. Any human with any kind of conscience could easily be affected negatively with guilt and remorse over the inhumane treatment I, and others like me, have received. It would do no good for me to be angry with them. Plus, it would not change anything for me even if everyone involved felt nothing. I think it would probably be good for them to see that the outcome of my life and its many accomplishments has proven that I am not "a waste of human life."

Medical mistakes happen in all hospital settings. It is the culture or policy within the Department of Veteran's affairs that forces staff to cover up their mistakes and avoid taking responsibility in the claims process. What needs to be called into question is the policy or motivation of those who issued the orders.

In moving on, it is to encourage employers and educators to see the value in people and what they have to offer in the job market and in society regardless or even in spite of a physical or mental disability.

It is about inspiring and motivating disabled people to have hope and be secure in the knowledge that they can set goals for themselves, not limitations!

It is to say that we do not have to accept limitations set down upon us by those who think they know what a person can or cannot accomplish because of a physical or mental disability.

CHAPTER 1:
AT THE CORPS

t was second night of the "World's Toughest Rowing Race" and we had over 2,550 nautical miles of Atlantic Ocean left to row. I was surrounded by miles of ink-black ocean, engulfed by pitch-black darkness. The winds increased and the sea exploded, sending wave after wave, invisible in the darkness, crashing down upon me. Being that low to the water with the waves thundering over the boat, there is always a risk of being knocked overboard or even of the whole boat capsizing. I wore my life jacket with the built-in harness, which was attached to the safety cable that ran the length of the boat. Nearing exhaustion after having rowed all day and half way through the night, I knew I was going to have to stop rowing and rest. But with no one being on the oar, the risk of capsizing in the unpredictable waves increases.

The conditions were so bad and I was so cold that I decided to put on my one-piece survival suit. Sitting on my rowing seat I struggled as the boat was violently tossed around. I managed to get both legs in and then it became necessary to remove my lifeline leaving myself unsecured. Immediately, I was struck by a big wave and was knocked up to and over the bow of the boat. The strap on my survival suit got hooked on the spare oar stanchion long enough for me to get a hand hold on the boat. I quickly secured my line to the cable and curled up at the bow with the suit only half-way on. This was my worst night of the trip but certainly not the worst night of my life. My life did not slowly flash before my eyes. Thinking about all that had transpired in my life leading up to this challenge was all I could do while huddled up on the bow of the boat not knowing if I would see another sunrise.

Born and raised in Ohio-the cornfields, cows, pigs, woodlands and creeks that surrounded my sister, five brothers and me, gave our lives a "Little House on the Prairie" sort of appearance. But my childhood wasn't exactly easy.

With so many brothers, it was normal to be considered "one of the boys" and I ended up being pretty good at most sports, fighting and defending myself; in fact, sucker punches from out of nowhere were pretty common. Early combat training! I excelled at sports all through high school – volleyball, softball and basketball, and had a scrapbook full of ribbons, medals, awards and countless newspaper articles. Sports motivated me to keep my grades up and kept me out of trouble, well not all trouble…

During my junior year in high school, I got pregnant and decided to keep the baby girl I named Jennifer when she was born in June of 1977. And I continued to play sports until I graduated a year later. There I was with a baby and a high school diploma and I asked myself, "Now what?" Although I was good enough at sports to get a volleyball scholarship to college, I tried Ohio State for Volleyball but was turned down because I was a single parent. They mistakenly believed that I would not be able to keep up with the practice schedule, be a full time student and be a single parent. I was never even given the opportunity to try.

In high school, I was a power hitter on the volleyball team, 1978

I had an especially wicked serve

I crossed college off of my list—a list that happened to include the Olympics. But with a new life that included a baby, I felt that I had to give up my Olympic dream and tried to set a more realistic goal.

As I look back, I don't know if I really planned on a military career or if it was something that was considered a logical next step in my life. My dad was a Navy veteran, my oldest brother was in the Navy and two other brothers were in the Marine Corps. My younger brother Clifford wanted to enlist in the Marine Corps so we enlisted together in April, 1979. Being a single parent, I had to get a waiver and accept an open contract when I enlisted. This meant that I was not permitted to choose my military occupational specialty but would be placed where they needed me. After my basic training at Paris Island, South Carolina, I was sent to Fort McClellan in Alabama for training as a Military Police officer. The Military Police Academy wasn't my idea. I was always interested in mechanical things and engineering. But good test scores and no criminal record made me a more qualified candidate for the roll of 5811(a specialty military occupation service number) or, in other words, Military Police.

The Academy was physical and I always excelled at anything and everything physical, I thoroughly enjoyed it.

A proud Marine in her uniform

After I graduated from the Military Academy, I was stationed in El Toro, California. Decommissioned in 1999, El Toro was the home of Marine Corps Aviation and could handle the largest military aircraft. (Probably the most little-known details about El Toro include the fact that the Marines were actually featured in the 1953 movie *The War Of The Worlds,* and between '57 and '59 Lee Harvey Oswald was stationed there as a radar operator). I loved being an MP and it was all going well.

I arranged for my base housing and had my daughter with me. I took up surfing and fell in love with the ocean, the Marine Corps & life.

I began playing basketball in my spare time for my El Toro Base recreational women's basketball team. I was good – damn good. The entire team excelled and after winning a number of games, our El Toro Women's Team went to the West Coast Regionals in Barstow, California and I was transferred to play on the Women's All-Marine Corps Basketball Team. I was back participating at a sport that I loved. It felt great and I was highly motivated. Okay, it wasn't the Olympics but the dream in me was alive and well and I was maintaining a physical state of combat readiness! My commanding officer was not a very willing participant in my transfer but the coach who outranked him insisted. I was 6' 1" tall, aggressive, very coordinated, and the best person for the job. I was selected to play center position.

All that changed during a simple practice game. As I went up for a rebound, someone tripped me; I fell forward, hit the floor and someone landed on top of my back. The paralysis and pain was immediate and shot through my entire body; it felt as if I had been struck by lightning. Players and coaches quickly surrounded me. My first reaction was to get up, shake it off and get back to the game. I tried to pull myself off the floor, but was unable to move my lower body. Everyone knew something serious had happened, but they were ill-equipped to treat me. I was transported to Camp Pendleton in Southern California. My parents were called and informed that not only had I been injured in an accident and suffered two ruptured discs and a damaged sciatic nerve, but the doctors did not know if I would ever walk again.

Now, you have to ask yourself – how can women who are supposedly trained Marines and elite athletes be so uncoordinated as to trip a player? One side of my brain said, "Accident." But the other side couldn't help but feel a little paranoid. I was an MP after all. Similar to the disdain many civilian police feel for the Internal Affairs department, most armed services members don't feel a particular affection for the military police. It was also the duty of the Military Police to report gays and lesbians. This was 1980, long before the "Don't Ask, Don't Tell" policy was enacted by President Clinton in 1993. If you were gay in the military you were considered "not fit for duty." (Unaware of my orientation when I enlisted and believing myself to be straight, I still didn't see the need to report anyone for being gay. I viewed the policy as being hypocritical. The oath I swore to God and country was to protect and defend all Americans both at home and abroad. I discovered I was gay during my service but dared not come out so my teammates had no idea.) Most of my fellow teammates were lesbians who didn't know about my orientation and were afraid that I would report them. In their minds, I'm sure that having me on the team put them at risk. Having a young child, being a single parent and having non-military male friends led everyone to believe that I was straight. I knew about my teammates but they did not know about me.

Back then, everyone was so fearful and afraid of being outed or falsely accused that it affected behavior. Everyone stayed to themselves and were forced to live very separate lives, fearful that they will come out to the wrong person and they'd be reported. Gays and lesbians who were open about their sexual orientation — or who were outed — faced punishment and expulsion.

So was there something sinister behind a practice game of b-ball? Was it a result of the policy of not allowing gays to serve openly and honestly? Did my commanding officer, harboring a grudge against my transfer, have something to do with it? Or was it just an old-fashioned, "oops, I'm sorry" accident? I'll never know for sure but what I did know was that I was in agonizing pain. It would begin in my lower back, radiate down my leg and travel all the way down to my toes. Fortunately, the initial prognosis of permanent paralysis from this incident did not materialize, although I had to temporarily use a wheelchair. Though the pain was unbearable, I learned to live with it. I worked hard in physical therapy and was able to recover enough to walk but basketball was out of the question. After being released from my orders to play ball for the Marine Corps, I returned to my unit, Released on light duty at El Toro three weeks after my hospitalization and ordered to continue to receive follow up care at my duty station.

After my release from the hospital, I knew that I could no longer meet the physical requirements of an MP; my career was over. I could no longer perform, let alone *pass* a PFT (a highly emphasized physical fitness test). My Commanding Officer had a reputation as a manipulator and I had already had a few run-ins with him. He would bring me into his office at the end of my shift and make me sit there while he made comments like "I do not have children" and "I have all night," while the people at the day care were waiting for me to pick up my daughter. At first I thought he was putting pressure on me to turn people in for being gay, asking me personal questions about everyone and about myself. But after my request, he let me know that the condition of my duty status and or my discharge could be determined by my willingness to do "certain things." He made inappropriate sexual remarks and his actions were offensive. He would brush his hand across the back of my shoulders and tell me how my life, "would be so much better if I cooperated" and that I knew what he wanted. His intentions were clear. More than once I got up and left his office under threat of disciplinary action. The more I resisted, the worse it got. When I received orders for a temporary assignment of duty to play basketball for the Women's All Marine Corps Basketball Team, he was livid. Now I was back and he made my life a living hell.

Not only would my commanding officer assign me jobs that were surely not light duty and constantly change my work schedule, but he would block my attempts to get medical care and rehabilitation for my service-related injuries and block and prevent me from getting medical care for my child.

I took my complaints to my Master Sergeant and asked to be transferred to another base or a change of duty or military occupational specialty. But my commanding officer denied my requests. I requested an occupational transfer to a job that was less physically challenging. Again, I was denied. I asked about a medical discharge, and was again denied. I said no, so he said no. According to my Commanding Officer, if I did not perform the "duties" he requested, then my only options were a Less Than Honorable Discharge or a Dishonorable Discharge. There was no way I was going to submit willfully to the options presented. He went so far as to change my schedule and then tried to have me detained and arrested at the gate charging me with unauthorized absence. My babysitter who was an MPs wife tipped me off. It was so dramatic, like right out of a movie and could not be really happening… or could it? Since my Master Sergeant could find no solution, I phoned the Headquarters legal department. I made arrangements to turn myself in to the officer there at the legal department. I took my daughter with me and went to the back gate by base housing. The Military Police officer at the gate was new and we did not know each other. He did try to stop me, I told him I had orders by an outranking officer to report to the legal department. He let me go. I made it about a half way there before I had MP vehicles following me trying to prevent me from reaching the headquarters building. My commanding officer did not want me to make it to legal and wanted to discipline me "In house". I did not stop and I did not break any regulations. They did not turn the lights on until I was 1 block from the building. I parked close to the door, got out of my car and quickly got my daughter out of her car seat. It happened so fast.

I had my back to the MP and I ignored his requests right up to the point where he raised his voice to shout PFC Madsen halt or I will fire, I thought I heard the sound of a shotgun being pumped, I lunged for the door. I had made it inside with my daughter safely. I reported all of the abuse and harassment to the Base Commander. The only solution he offered me was a Hardship Discharge. Well, I thought, at least it would be a discharge under honorable conditions; I submitted, under duress, as I saw no other options. I was young and naïve. I thought I had gone as far up the chain of command as possible, and that this was my final option. Take it or leave it. So I took it.

I wasn't in any position to turn it down. Now, all these years later, I finally know better. It was the Marine Corps' way of washing over the sexual harassment. Incorporated in the health care system at the VA hospitals are sexual trauma counselors to help women deal with the sexual abuse they encounter during their service to our country; I was so naïve at the time, I didn't even know I had someone else to turn to.

In the meantime, I was transferred to the civilian fire station on base, where I performed secretarial work until my discharge had been processed. My Commanding Officer continued to harass other females in the unit but was ordered to stay away from me. Although I received an Honorable discharge, I was not allowed to discuss the circumstances of my discharge and he could no longer cause me any harm, so I thought.

The legal department made all of the arrangements, from obtaining statements (true and untrue) from people associated with me to obtaining statements regarding the inability of my parents to take custody of my daughter. Legal told people what I needed to have on paper to make a good case for a hardship discharge, and they did it. I complied, too.

———

There was enough documentation and confirmed diagnoses at the time to warrant an evaluation for a Medical Discharge. I did not find out until 1993, fourteen years later, that the statement, "Line of duty and misconduct status undetermined" was written in my records and may have lead to the medical discharge process being halted and denied. My DD214 (Official discharge paper) seems to contradict those words as it says that I received a good conduct award and was given a hardship discharge. I am not aware of the details of who, when and how the "misconduct status undetermined" was added to my file. It could have been my commanding officers doing or it could have been added years later by someone adjudicating my claim for Veterans benefits. It does not matter. The result and damage it has done would be the same either way.

There was no misconduct involved in my injury. I played basketball for the Women's All-Marine Basketball Team. I was under orders, on duty, and doing my job. I went up for a rebound during a practice game. I was tripped and someone landed on my back. I fail to see how anyone could conceive misconduct from what happened. So why is that statement there? Was it my Commanding Officer because I refused to have sex with him? Was it the Legal Department at the base trying to justify the circumstances of my non-medical discharge and their cover up of the sexual harassment? It's another mystery.

Eventually, I did win my case and did receive the correct disability rating and all of my benefits; however, this does not change the type of discharge I received nor does it remove the false accusation or implication of misconduct in my file. It has taken me a long time to come to terms with the circumstances surrounding my discharge. I did what many women do under the circumstances. I was open and honest about it at base legal and I was punished for it by being wrongfully discharged. My Commanding Officer not only was able to continue to engage in conduct unbecoming, he continued to receive promotions.

My discharge should have been a Medical Discharge – but I felt as long as it was under honorable conditions it would be okay. It wasn't. I had two ruptured disc which caused difficulty walking, sitting and standing for any period of time—I couldn't lift anything or perform tasks needed to be employable. I could not get medical care from the VA because my discharge was not medical. I had trouble finding a job because of my medical condition. It was bad enough being physically broken, 3,000 miles from my home with my daughter, and knowing that a Dishonorable Discharge would make me even more unemployable than my medical condition had made me. How would I have a future raising and providing for my daughter? *Welfare?* I don't think so! This man thought he could use his power over me to make me do whatever he wanted. I don't think so!

In 1981, at the age of twenty-one, I was honorably, but wrongfully, discharged from the Marine Corps.

CHAPTER 2:
WALKING IN,
WHEELING OUT

With nowhere to go and a toddler in tow, I decided to make Southern California my home. I eventually found work and even though I had initially used a wheelchair, I ultimately recovered enough to walk and play some recreational volleyball in the park every Sunday. Since I was so near to the ocean, I learned how to surf. There's nothing like walking through the warm sand, diving in the cold waters of the Pacific and climbing on top of a board and letting nature take you for a ride. I put competing in a major surf contest on my to do list.

I improved enough to go after my life goal of doing something mechanical and even though the job was physically demanding and tough on my back, I became a mechanic for Sears in the automotive department. The work was strenuous and the pain was barely tolerable but I managed to hold down that job for six years. I later had a similar job at U-Haul. Two very demanding, physical jobs, but I worked hard despite the pain. For years, I refused to believe that there were things I couldn't handle or work through. I had always lived by the "pull yourself up by your bootstraps" ethic but little did I know that one of the first signs of adjustment disorder is ignoring the in-your-face facts of a given situation. I managed to avoid the wheelchair up to that point; but the day came when I finally realized that not only did I have to give up any kind of physical job, but competitive sports as well. Eventually, it got to the point that I could not work at all.

You know, it's hard to give up something you have known your entire life. Physically demanding and satisfying work, playing sports, or even going for a walk takes a lot out of a person's body and, at that moment in my life, I felt like I didn't have a body. We don't have to tell our right leg, "Go forward." It's something we do that's natural. Our bodies are on automatic pilot and mine was shorting out. I had always defined myself as an athlete and an able-bodied hard worker. I had to take a look at myself and ask, "Who am I? What else am I good for?" I had to work, to take care of my daughter.

Since I always enjoyed mechanical engineering and wrenching on things, I enrolled in MTI College in the City of Orange and became a computer-aided drafter. I went from repairing machines to designing them. It was a good fit.

After my certification, I found a great job designing and detailing high-speed pneumatic labeling machines at a firm that didn't care about my sexual orientation or my disability; I finally felt like "this was it!" The universe had shifted in my favor. I was able to utilize my mechanical ability without making the physical demands on my body. I excelled at what I did so much that my company considered sending me to school for a degree in mechanical engineering. I had a great working relationship with everyone at work and life was going great. I had it all. A career, a future…I was on top of the world!

Family life continued to have challenges that could not be solved by having a good career. Jennifer, by now 14 years old, had, for years, been exhibiting frantic mood swings, bouts of sleeplessness, and would explode into unexplained rages-far beyond the range of "normal" adolescent angst.

She had always been a moody child and I associated her behavior to my erratic employment and financial hardships and I felt guilty at not being able to provide a better life for her. More than once, because of my constant intense back pain and mobility limitations, we were forced to live our lives in areas and in situations that were far from ideal; we even lived in a garage for a year. To avoid being homeless, I had to take in a roommate most of the time to help share expenses. The endless parade of people coming and going, I thought, was too much for her to handle. She'd medicate herself with drugs and alcohol, hang out with the wrong people and get into trouble. I blamed myself, of course, and tried everything to ease whatever pain I thought she was suffering. But my love for her wasn't enough; she ran away from home, the first of many escapes she would make from my life.

In 1992, in the midst of my deteriorating relationship with my daughter, I was in a car accident. My little Volkswagen Bug and I were heading out for a day at the beach when a driver, still appearing drunk from the night before or asleep at the wheel, was speeding down the middle of my street and hit me head on. When the police arrived, I heard the driver tell them that he was a parole officer and that he had taken my street as a shortcut to beat the light because he was late for church. You should have seen the understanding looks on their faces; needless to say, he was treated with the utmost respect.

I sustained numerous injuries from the accident – I broke my wrist, my leg, and some ribs. The combination of my injuries prevented me from being able to use crutches and once again, I had to use a wheelchair "temporarily" for ambulation.

Miraculously, I managed to miss only two days from work. Unable to drive, my supervisor would pick me up in Long Beach every day and take me to work. Once I recovered, I again made a hasty exit from the wheelchair. It would take more than a few injuries to prevent me from hanging on to my seemingly able-bodied life as I knew it. Years later, I learned that I was actually suffering from adjustment disorder; I was denying my disability and having difficulty accepting the limitations from my disability. Adjustment disorder occurs when a person is unable to cope with, or adjust to, a particular source of stress, such as a major life change, loss, or event.

The injuries, and my inability to remain physically active through the recovery, accelerated the deterioration of my spinal condition from my accident in the Corps. In fact, the spinal degeneration was so severe that surgery became inevitable. I was finding it necessary to again utilize a wheelchair temporarily for ambulation. While I was receiving treatment and being diagnosed for my spinal injury at UCI Medical Center in Irvine, the hospital learned that my initial injury occurred while I was in the Marines.

The night before my scheduled surgery, I received a call from the hospital, "We're sorry. All of the tests indicate that you had two desiccated discs and major spinal degeneration that was indicative of previous injury sustained while you were in the military. Your insurance company refuses to pay for your surgery or rehabilitation." They suggested I should go to the Veterans Hospital in Long Beach for treatment. I had no idea what was in store for me.

Veterans Hospitals, like so many other hospitals, are teaching hospitals and I have mentioned this previously but there are some other major differences. Care of specific service related conditions, sources of funding and the disability claims process are unlike the other educational hospitals. Veterans Hospitals are also federally protected from law suits and when politicians cut VA medical budgets or do not pass bills for additional veteran hospital funding, they really are depriving the students of the best education possible—and depriving veterans of the best care.

Making sure veterans have everything they need must be a priority and people should realize and respect veterans for their continued service to their country. Every member of the Armed Forces takes an oath of service to defend and protect the rights and freedoms for all Americans at home and abroad. It is our job, our duty. We are promised medical care and benefits for our service. I did not create the system for medical care at the Veteran hospitals nor is it any veteran's fault that the education our doctors receive is sub par or inadequate; it's everyone's. To improve the quality of health care for everyone (including veterans) we should all become proactive. We all have opportunities and responsibilities to help secure the necessary funding or to keep politicians from cutting the funding to veterans hospitals. It has nothing to do with supporting a war or the troops; rather, it is an investment in the doctors and nurses who train there. Because, eventually, the VA doctors make their way to your hospital, clinic or medical center and you'll be their patient.

After my examination at the Veterans Medical Center it was determined that I required spinal surgery: a posterior and anterior fusion of two levels of the lumbar region of my lower back at L3-L4 and L4-L5. The spinal column, which extends from the skull to the pelvis, is made up of thirty-three individual bones. The bones of the lumbar region are stacked on top of each other and numbered 1 through 5 and curve along your lower back. Bone graft from my hip would replace my discs and metal Herrington rods and screws would stabilize the spinal column until it healed.

Knowing I was eligible and in need of a wheelchair I went to see the patient representative and in turn, followed up with the Acting Chief of Prosthetics, regarding my eligibility requirements. After going through a checklist, and confirming that I met all the criteria, an order for my permanent lightweight wheelchair was submitted. Not only was this order for the wheelchair, but it also included all of the other things I would need once I was released and recuperating at home: a raised toilet seat with rails, a shower seat, hand-held shower fixture, and a cushion for the wheelchair. The Acting Chief of Prosthetics denied the order. The patient representative called prosthetics and informed them again that I met all the criteria, from "need" to eligibility. The Acting Chief of Prosthetics still objected, and when I resubmitted the request, he huffed and puffed, making it clear that he was only going to partially comply with the order. Later, he only approved an order for a temporary chair, a raised toilet seat, and the chair cushion. That was it. For all the things I did get, the list of things I didn't – but needed – was just as long: I didn't receive an appointment to the wheelchair clinic for a lightweight wheelchair; I didn't receive handrails for the toilet or the shower seat nor did I receive the hand-held shower fixture. I watched the Acting Chief of Prosthetics deliberately pick and choose what he thought I needed, totally disregarding the physician's orders.

I know what you're probably asking yourself and the answer is "No," this man was not medically qualified to make the decisions he made regarding my requests. Since I met all the criteria, I should have received everything on the request form. I did manage to get a loaner wheelchair for temporary use. But that was it.

After this demoralizing episode, I decided to wait until after my surgery to pursue the remaining items; by that time, I thought, the powers that be would have reevaluated my request and would furnish everything that I needed.

So on August 26, 1993, I was admitted to the VA Medical Center for spinal surgery. "Good," I thought, "let's get this over with" – I want to get back to work, get back to the beach, and play a game of basketball or two. Although now I realize it was part of my adjustment disorder, I refused to believe the seriousness of my condition and insisted that I would be walking and surfing again within a year and that at the most I would miss three weeks more of work.

The following day, I was prepped and anesthetized, and taken to the operating room at 7:30 a.m. The surgeons completed the operation approximately seven hours later and afterwards I was taken to ICU. When I awoke, I was in *extreme* pain. I could not move and could not lift myself to get onto a bedpan without screaming in agony.

After an overnight stay in ICU, I was transferred to a recovery ward. Days later, I was still experiencing an extraordinary amount of pain and I still could not move. The doctors ordered X-rays, which showed that my upper level bone graft had moved forward and had been dislodged somehow either when I was being moved from the operating room to ICU or it was not properly installed to begin with. And that wasn't the worst of it. The doctors told me that they had mistakenly fused three levels instead of two.

However, the team of doctors assured me that the dislodged bone would be repaired in the next surgery. In the meantime, I was ordered to lay still and move as little as possible so the dislocated bone wouldn't move. To keep the bone from slipping further or creating additional damage, I was confined to strict bed rest.

I followed the doctor's instructions and stayed as immobile as possible. I was in such extreme pain that I would wake up screaming in the middle of the night. Even the slightest movement was unbearable. The nurses on the ward didn't want to touch me; in fact, they were afraid to assist me because of the immense amount of pain that every little movement caused, and because of the highly emphasized instability of the shifted bone graft.

Two weeks passed, and on September 10th, at 7:30 am, I was taken to the operating room for my second surgery. Once again, I was prepped and anesthetized. But this time, the surgery took about ten hours – five hours longer than anyone expected. Afterwards, I was taken to ICU, where I woke up with two drains in my back, located on each side of the incision. I was draining copious amounts of fluid and every hour the nurses would take turns emptying both drainage bottles. An analysis of the fluid later showed that it was cerebrospinal fluid (CSF), which acts like a cushion, protecting the brain and spine. The brain floats in it. So it was no surprise that the loss of spinal fluid would lead to painful spinal headaches.

The fluid leak remained constant, but on the last day of my stay in ICU, the fluid draining from the left side gradually started to slow down slightly and I was transferred back to a recovery ward. After about seven days, the drainage on the left side decreased enough for the doctors to be able to remove the drainage bottle, and the fluid in the remaining drain was monitored. It drained heavily and constantly for the next few days.

Then the doctor told me they would have to perform another surgery to repair a tear in the thecal sac, which is a membrane that surrounds the spinal cord and circulates cerebral spinal fluid. Only they never surgically repaired it. The doctor removed the drain, put a thick elastic pressure bandage on my back, and inverted my bed approximately fifteen degrees in the Trendelenburg position, so my body had to lay with my feet higher than my head.

I remained in that inverted position for 24 hours a day. Sleeping, eating, and using a bedpan, while having your head lower than your feet is no easy task. It was so difficult to swallow while inverted that I would choke when I tried to eat or drink anything. Then, I started getting nosebleeds. As the spinal headaches began to lessen, my bed was adjusted little by little to a flatter position. At this point, I had only mild headaches and eventually I was allowed to sit up. When my headaches remained mild, they transferred me to B-1, the post-op and orthopedic rehabilitation ward. In total, my CSF leaked for twelve days. I couldn't help but wonder if there would be any residual or long-term effects from having such a severe spinal fluid leak for such a lengthy period of time.

An intern, explained to me that the instrumentation they used works for about 90% of the patients who have this surgery. The surgery had to be performed manually instead of by the standard pre-set method that works for most patients. My surgery was totally botched—he explained that the doctors removed the wrong disc at the wrong level which made it necessary to fuse another level. They then had to hustle to Los Angeles to try to locate the specific additional hardware. Then they installed the rods and crossbars out of sequence, and they had to take it all apart and start over. In the second surgery they neglected to repair the loose bone fragments and bone grafts that were installed improperly during the first surgery. The intern went on to explain that all three bone grafts were wedged on the left side rather than centralized, and the upper one was sticking out, causing an aortic impingement, which could require further surgery.

Shortly after I arrived at B-1, I was sent to physical therapy but it was a case of too much, too soon. The intensity of the headaches began to increase again and I was experiencing urinary tract pain. I was positive that I had developed a urinary tract infection (UTI). I shared my complaints with my rehab doctor, but he gave me very little regard and did nothing for me. Because the rehabilitation doctor would not treat my urinary tract infection, I had to ask my orthopedic doctor, for help. He also made it clear that I had to take it easy on the physical therapy.

Unfortunately, rehab medicine did not agree with my orthopedic doctor and before I knew it, rehab had *increased* my physical therapy rather than decrease it, as the doctor had advised. In addition to forcing me to do more therapy than I was physically able to handle, the appointments were scheduled so tightly throughout the hospital that I could not possibly get to all of them on time. Plus, there was no time for me to lie down and get a little bit of badly-needed pain relief in between therapies. To make things even worse, rehab chose to cut down on my pain medication, which only increased my pain level and decreased the progress of my rehabilitation.

With a lot of juggling, cajoling and anger on my part, I got my therapy appointments arranged so that I had two appointments in the morning, two in the afternoon, and two hours in-between to rest; and even then, I was still having the painful headaches. Then I learned more details of how badly the doctors screwed up the second surgery.

They told me that they knew they placed a screw questionably close or through the dural sac and ruptured it, causing the spinal fluid leak and spinal cord injury. They said that not only did the screw cause the continual headaches, but it was the reason why I could potentially need another surgery. What? Was I in some sort of Twilight Zone? Hundreds of questions roared into my head. If they knew the screw was too close or even inserted through my spinal cord, why did they leave it that way? Why didn't they repair it before they closed me up? If they knew I had a spinal fluid leak and a torn Dural sac, why didn't they repair it?

In the case of the second surgery, the surgeon should have noticed all of the conditions they described from the previous X-rays, MRI and CT scan. Everyone had two weeks between my surgeries to prepare and get the correct instrumentation. The alleged conditions that made it necessary for the doctors to fuse three levels in the first surgery were the same conditions which caused the complications with instrumentation – spine curvature and disc degeneration.

It was clear that they were lying to me about some things and speaking small truths about others.

What about the screw that was resting so dangerously close to my spinal cord? Did they remove the loose bone fragments? What about my intensely throbbing reoccurring spinal headaches? What, if any, neurological changes should I expect?

When the doctors finally came around to talk to me, all I heard was, "Spinal column…pierced…partially paralyzed…waist down. You won't be able to walk again for a year or two, maybe never."

What??! I walked in for a seemingly routine procedure to fuse two levels of my spine to prevent paralysis but I'd be leaving a paraplegic?! In addition to feeling hopeless and helpless, I was angry.

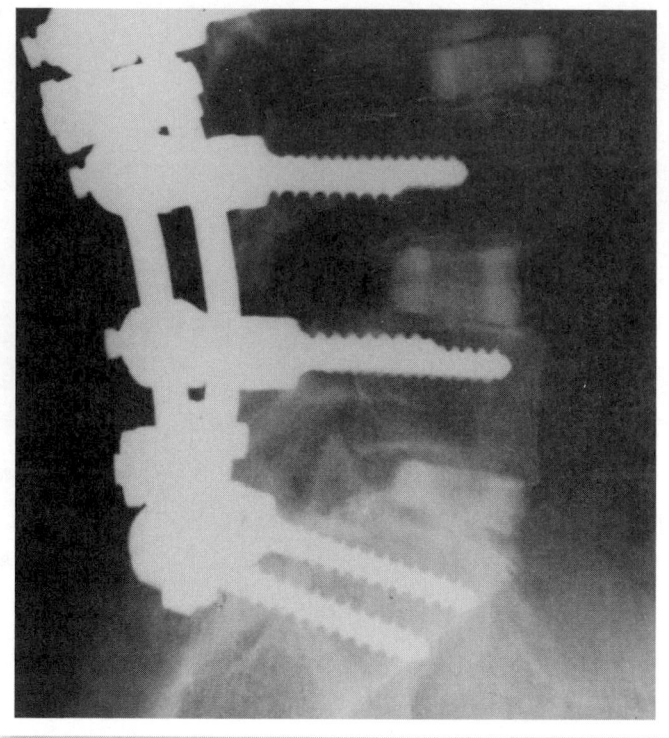

X-ray side view of the hardware in my back

In my follow-up appointment in orthopedics for X-rays, I was told that I would have to have X-rays once a month for an uncertain amount of time. I didn't understand why until after I saw those X-rays – there was a bone graft, clearly sticking out. I was furious. That was the bone they told me they were going to fix or repair during the second surgery when they repaired the bone grafts! Now I was being told that I would have to have X-rays all the time to make sure that the bone doesn't move!?

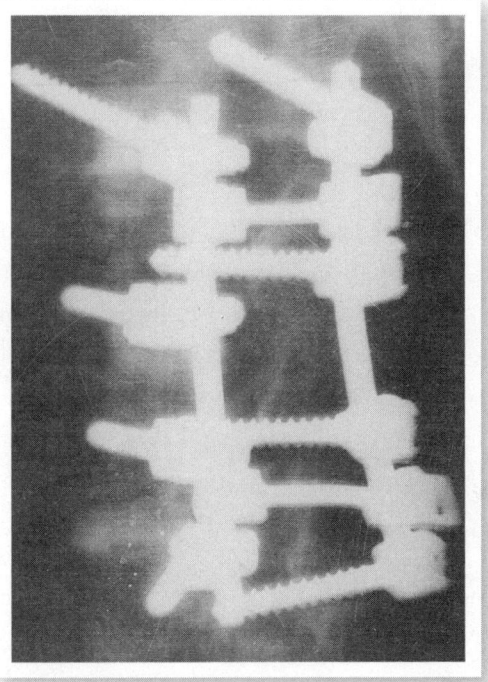

X-ray oblique view

My pounding head kept repeating the same questions: How long would this take? How safe was I, and what happened "if"? I was afraid to get out of bed, afraid of falling or injuring myself. Could this be the cause of all the pain I was having? If something had to be done about the bone, would it be better to wait? I made the decision that I needed to see my records, and needed to get another opinion about the bone graft. I continued to express concern over this in my therapies and with the rehab doctors, but they continued to give me the impression that they could care less about my fears and concerns. Plus, they kept treating me like I was just another chronic pain patient, not an acute pain patient. I was beginning to think they didn't know the difference. (Chronic pain progresses over a long period of time and is often resistant to medical treatment whereas acute pain can come on quickly and last for only a short time).

After my surgeries, and in light of all the complications that occurred, the orthopedic surgeon performed yet another evaluation and submitted another request for a permanent-issue lightweight wheelchair. Somehow, this request was lost in Prosthetics, and nothing was ever heard about it again.

By now, I had been in the hospital for eight weeks, and had suffered through two unsuccessful surgeries. Then I was given my discharge notice. But I wasn't ready or able to take care of myself. Plus, I hadn't figured out how I was going to get to my therapy appointments after my release. I kept asking myself, "What am I going to do? I don't know how to take care of myself being in a wheelchair and being this disabled!"

The lightweight wheelchair became an issue once more when I was being discharged from the hospital. A doctor from the rehabilitation department wrote a request, and I hand-carried it to Prosthetics. A social worker on my ward specifically stated that since I was an outpatient, I would receive a lightweight wheelchair and assured me that I would receive one in approximately a week and a half. Not only was I promised that I would be able to continue my physical therapy, but also that the VA travel department would provide transportation to and from my appointments.

Despite the fact I was physically unable to care for myself, I was discharged under protest from the V.A.M.C. on October 25, 1993. The doctors at the VA assumed that just because I shared an apartment with someone that the other person would take care of me.

For a week and a half following my discharge, I received no physical therapy. I contacted my California Congressman's office, hoping for some sort of advocacy support. She made a few phone calls, but later told me that the VA doctors had explained to her that I was "ambulatory with hand crutches," could walk 150 feet, and that a lightweight wheelchair had been ordered for me and would arrive in a week.

It seemed clear to me that she believed what the VA had told her, and in the process they made me look like I wasn't credible and that maybe I was just looking for attention. Obviously, I was disappointed that she had taken the word of VA employees who were desperately trying to cover their rears over mine – like I had something to gain by "crying wolf." I felt frustrated, betrayed, and powerless … again.

Being home alone was discouraging, humiliating, embarrassing, dehumanizing, lonely, and above all dangerous. I could barely manage, although I don't know how. When I asked my roommate to do something for me, she responded resentfully. She had been counseled at work a few times for being constantly late because she was trying to help me by chauffeuring me to appointments or helping me get started on my day. She told me she felt guilty about having to leave me alone all the time, and at times, she expressed as much frustration, or perhaps even more frustration, with the VA system and my disability, than I did. It was creating a lot of stress between us. I found that relationships and friendships do not usually survive disability. Being newly-disabled, you have to start over in so many more ways than people realize—or at least in far more ways than I would have ever imagined.

CHAPTER 3:
FOLLOW UPS, LET DOWNS

was far from "ambulatory." The big, bulky, temporary wheelchair they issued me could not fit through the bathroom door of the apartment. One day, while attempting to squeeze and wiggle my way to the toilet, I fell flat on the floor. I couldn't get up—I couldn't even crawl. I lay there helpless for four agonizing hours until my roommate got home from work and helped me up off the floor. I spent the next week recuperating in bed because I was afraid that I would injure myself getting up again. I was too scared to even attempt another trip to the bathroom. And with my incontinence problems after the surgery, let's just say that a box of Depends became a standard piece of equipment.

Two weeks after my discharge, I went back to the VA Medical Center for a follow-up appointment with my orthopedic surgeon. Needless to say, there was no lightweight wheelchair waiting for me when I checked in at prosthetics. In fact, I was informed that no order for a wheelchair had ever been made, which completely contradicted what the Congressman's office was told. I was told that it would be impossible for them to order a chair for me without going through the wheelchair clinic first.

My next attempt to get my doctor-ordered wheelchair sent me to the Office of Consumer Affairs. The Consumer Affair's patient representative assisted me in obtaining an appointment for the wheelchair clinic. "Okay," I thought, "now I'll get the wheelchair." Everything was set and an appointment was scheduled. Only one problem – nobody notified me.

I later returned to the Office of Consumer Affairs Patient Representative, only to find out that I had missed it! It seemed like this was a tactic they used to label the patient as a no show and uncooperative.

I went to see my rehab doctor, who scheduled my outpatient therapy to begin the following Monday. "Okay," I thought, "at least now I'll get my physical therapy."

But the VA Travel office was closed for the weekend and I couldn't make an appointment with travel for a Monday pick up, so I had to endure a long, rough, painful bus ride to my therapy.

I arrived at the VA only to find out that they wouldn't treat me because the therapist hadn't received written orders from the doctor. I was in agony from being bounced around on the bus, and then to find out that I had done it all for nothing? I immediately filed a Report of Contact (complaint) on the doctor. The office assured me that that the written orders would be taken care of and I would be treated on Wednesday. Luckily, a friend picked me up and took me home. The following day, I called VA Travel to make sure I would have transportation to my therapy appointments on that Wednesday. But I was told that I was not eligible for VA Travel; I was denied.

Was I getting the runaround for some reason? Was it personal? Or was every patient treated this way? With nothing to lose, I paid a visit to my Congressman's office in person and spoke with the staff person I had previously been speaking to. She was very supportive and helpful in assisting me with getting transportation from the VA.

As it turned out, my eligibility wasn't the problem. VA Travel hadn't even received the written orders or travel papers required to determine my eligibility. And whose responsibility was this? Answer: the Rehab Medicine doctor.

Why didn't someone in VA Travel tell me that travel papers hadn't been submitted when I spoke to them on the phone!? I was told verbatim that I was not eligible; they didn't say anything else. If they had told me what they really needed, I could have made a simple phone call and arranged to have the Rehab doctor submit the travel papers to them. It wouldn't have been necessary at all to involve my Congressman's office!

The whole situation hardly seemed right to me. First, I was discharged even though I was unable to care for myself. Second, after having two major surgeries for a service-connected condition, I was ineligible for VA Travel....WHY? Was it that the doctor had forgotten? Or maybe he was too lazy? Or had been instructed not to submit the request? I really do not know.

See any kind of pattern here? I tried not to take any of this personally; I had a pretty good hunch that all VA patients were treated this way. At last, after more hassles than anyone should have to endure, I finally had my fought-for outpatient therapies scheduled for three days a week – every Monday, Wednesday, and Friday. And I had VA transportation. Unfortunately, I still didn't have my promised lightweight wheelchair, so I was still unable to pull my weight around the house. So there I sat, home alone fearful, and unable to go anywhere except to my therapy appointments. Still relying on Depends or pads for my incontinence problems and being unable to change them myself. Still unable to twist and reach back far enough to wipe myself adequately when using the bathroom. My personal hygiene was horrible and I was unable to shower. Still unable to cook, do laundry, housework, or any other of the thousand and one things that we all need to do every minute of every day. And still the doctors had assured the Congressman's staff that I was "ambulatory with hand crutches."

Since the wheelchair couldn't fit in the bathroom, I tried to use hand crutches for the few steps to the toilet. I was constantly falling. I didn't notice that there was water on the bathroom floor and one of the hand-crutches just slipped out from under me and I took a nosedive onto the floor.

I was immediately rushed back to the VA and discussed my fears and concerns with an attending physician; but he took no X-rays, and only prescribed Robaxin, which is nothing more than a muscle relaxant. When I left, I was still in a horrible amount of pain and began losing the feeling in my right arm. The pain was just below my shoulders, and in my back. I was also having an odd feeling of nausea. Had the fall made the bone graft slip and move forward?

Not only was I concerned about the pain and the possibility that the bone had shifted, but I could feel that the bone was putting pressure on something internally.

The increasing pain was making it even more difficult for me to push my heavy wheelchair around the hospital. It was a huge complex and I had a great deal of ground to cover in a short amount of time so I began using the escort service on an outpatient-basis to get from appointment to appointment. It helped save my arms for the curbs, hills, and carpeting that I had to navigate, just to get into and around my inaccessible apartment. I began experiencing a lot of pain in both of my wrists and elbows since I'd been attempting to use the hand-crutches and pushing that heavy wheelchair. When I complained about the pain at one of my appointments, the attending doctor told me, "Rehab Medicine is supposed to treat you for this." He prescribed Motrin and sent me on my way.

Then, I began to wonder... was I losing my ability to push this particular wheelchair, or would I have problems with any chair? Was a lightweight chair really going to be that much easier to push? I knew that my friends and family would be more than willing to take me places if they could lift that heavy chair and load it into the car but if the condition in my arms continued to escalate, I knew I wouldn't be able to push a wheelchair, no matter how lightweight it was.

Sensing further problems with the wheelchair clinic, I involved my Disabled American Veteran's representative. We arrived at my wheelchair clinic appointment and met with a doctor who stated that, after reviewing my, files, I was being denied once again.

Carpal tunnel syndrome, two operations performed on my left wrist, or even my previous knee surgeries (in which I was diagnosed with chondromalacia of the patella, a degeneration of cartilage in the knee) were all legitimate reasons to prescribe and authorize a lightweight wheelchair and they were documented in my medical records. To make matters worse, the knee problem and leg pains I was experiencing at this time were actually nerve pain related to my spinal cord injury.

After the doctor proved to be so poorly informed about my medical history, I came to the conclusion that she had not actually read my records. When I questioned her about it, she replied, "Patients ask doctors for things such as wheelchairs, and doctors just fill out the request. Then I have to deny them. I am sorry." What was she saying about VA doctors? That was a pretty negative thing to say about any VA doctor's judgment and integrity. It was time to leave, as it was clear her mind was made up, and all the relevant information in the world wasn't going to change it.

The Disabled American Veteran's representative set up a meeting between the director of the hospital and the chief of prosthetics to try and resolve this wheelchair matter. By this time, I was getting pretty tired of the constant battles—no service-connected veteran having surgery for his or her service-connected disability should ever have to go through this. Surprisingly, I had a feeling that there would be a positive outcome – but I didn't want to have expectations one way or another, win or lose

There were some good people at the VA Hospital; people who treated me like a human being, and not just another service person's claim number. The trouble was (and probably still is), there just weren't enough of them.

Eventually, the VA began providing me with transportation to my medical appointments. With all of my countless trips to and from the Medical Center, I got to know some of the cab drivers and I actually looked forward to the rides. The cabbies liked coming to get me, and they never complained about helping me or lifting my heavy wheelchair. They didn't seem to be inconvenienced by me at all. They would even stop and get coffee for me in the morning sometimes and one of them even brought me a travel cup for our rides on the road. They seemed to actually like and care about me. I couldn't request any specific driver, but I would always ask for one in particular to try and get my fare. It seemed like this was the only good thing going for me. It felt good to be treated with respect for a change.

C H A P T E R 4 :
A N O T H E R
A C C I D E N T

On December 7, 1993, the universe came around one more time to kick me in the ass. (Is it written down somewhere that Angela is a synonym for Accident?)

I had yet another accident on my way out to the carport, just a few feet from my apartment. I headed out the front door and turned my wheelchair towards the sidewalk, which was downhill with a curb at the end. I started to slide then went into a speeding free fall. I careened off of the curb, then the footpads went over and bottomed out, the chair lunged forward and I was thrown from my wheelchair. Incapable of getting up, I waited until a passerby called 911. The medics came first, then the ambulance. As they took my vitals and placed me on the gurney, I immediately informed them about my post-op status and physical condition and asked them to transport me to V.A.M.C., but, they could not transport me and took me to the closest Medical Center.

The attendants in the emergency room quickly gave me medication for my pain and swiftly took X-rays. Nothing was broken, I was told, but they couldn't assess any other kind of damage without previous X-rays for comparison. When I mentioned that they could retrieve my X-rays from V.A.M.C, I was quickly discharged and told that I could be transported to the VA or to my home.

From the rushed treatment I received, it was obvious to me that they did not want to get involved with my medical treatment when I mentioned the "V" word. It was like I had suddenly contracted leprosy or something. And now, all of a sudden, they just wanted to get rid of me, without liability. One minute, they were considering admitting me, and the next minute I became a liability, a service-connected veteran with no insurance.

I phoned the emergency room at the VA and explained to the ER nurse that I was a post-op VA patient, gave her some of my medical history and informed her of what had happened and how I was injured.

Although the nurse spent a great deal of time on the phone with me, she was not sympathetic. I was injured and needed medical attention, I told her. In my present condition, it was impossible for me to go home. I certainly was not able to care for myself. Her responses ranged from, "Well, why didn't you see the social worker?" to "Why didn't you apply for welfare?" The entire conversation was more of what I had come to expect from the V.A.M.C. After clearly seeing that the conversation was going nowhere, I hung up. The medical center called an ambulance for me and transported me to the VA.

By the time I arrived at the VA Emergency room, I didn't know what time it was or what doctor I saw but I was in so much pain and so frustrated that I would have quite possibly killed myself if I had the opportunity. Once I voiced my concern that I had no one at home to help me, one of the E.R. nurses responded, "You are not going to be admitted just because you have no help at home!"

Looking back on it, I think it never should have gone that far. I should have had a physical examination. All the VA doctor did was ask me questions. When I answered, "Yes, the medical center took X-rays and nothing was broken," it didn't matter to him that I was in so much pain that I could not move and that I sustained an injury severe enough to warrant hospitalization.

None of this mattered to the doctor.... the thought of being home alone in this condition was just unacceptable to me. The pain was too unbearable. I was given nothing for my pain, they didn't examine me, and they didn't take X-rays. The doctor put me on bed-rest, telling me that if I experienced any loss of feeling or incontinence that I should return to the

ER. That's what I was there for! They asked me if I would like an ambulance instead of a taxi to transport me to my therapy the next day...I went home in an ambulance.

The following morning, another ambulance came and picked me up and I arrived at the VA in the same condition as the night before, except that the pain medication they gave me at the medical center had completely worn off and I was physically and emotionally drained. Therapy? I didn't think so. I couldn't even get into a wheelchair.

As they wheeled me into the ER, I was so angry, frustrated and exhausted from the previous evening that I automatically anticipated more of the same treatment. I wasn't about to start all over, so I took up where I left off. Soon, one thing led to another, and, still very worked up from the night before, I went into, what you might say, sort of an emotional frenzy. I thought for sure they were going to jerk me around again. To my disbelief and relief, they didn't.

When a doctor I had never seen before approached me, I was ready for a fight. However, when I explained what had happened, he simply said that different doctors do things differently. Then he talked to me, examined me, and admitted me. I don't know who he was, but I'd like to thank him.

Getting me admitted was no easy task. No one could find me a bed. The remaining rooms set aside for female patients were male occupied. At the VA, there is a significant lack of private rooms with bathrooms and showers for female patients. Many times women are forced to share the facilities with men. If a woman is lucky enough to get a room with a toilet and shower, her space and privacy are not respected. I saw nurses dump urine bottles in the women's bathroom at all hours of the day and night. They'd splash the contents over the floor and toilet including the seat. It was like sharing the bathroom with twenty or thirty men!

That's when the game of "ping-pong Angela" started. With no place to go, the ER doctor sent me to see a doctor in Rehab to possibly have me admitted to B1, the post op rehab ward; however, all the rooms set aside for female patients were also occupied and I was sent back to the ER.

So what happens to a female patient when there's no room at the inn? I spent hours lying on a gurney outside the ER while this kind-hearted doctor tried to find a place for me. At 6 pm that evening, I was finally admitted in the polio patient section —back in the same ward that I was stuck in after my failed surgeries. Months earlier, I shared that room with a stroke patient who fell in the bathroom and got feces on the floor; I looked at the floor and noted that it looked as though it hadn't been mopped since I was last hospitalized—perhaps it hadn't.

Later, I learned that Rehab doctor I had been dealing with had left, which sounds great, but he wasn't the only one I had problems with. He had a boss; someone who had to account for his errors. His boss disfavored me personally because someone called Congressman Royce's office on my behalf during my last admission. There was definite tension in that ward, and I felt awkward and uneasy most of the time. There was also a social worker who was not helpful.

The medical staff refused to give me pain meds, even though my orthopedic doctor prescribed them for me. After four days of excruciatingly painful, sleepless nights, they still refused to give me any medication for the pain. B1 was a ward for chronic pain patients, not for post-operative acute pain patients like me. I knew and they knew that I didn't belong in that ward, but they were not going to change protocol.

The constant pain caused sleep deprivation, which left my mind muddled; I must have seemed a little dazed and confused because someone from the psychiatric department visited me more than once. My doctor from rehabilitation told me that I may get transferred to the "loony lounge," but when I asked the psychiatrist who visited me about a transfer, he knew nothing about it. He also assured me that no one in his department had made the recommendation, nor had they discussed my case with the physicians (because I had requested patient confidentiality). So what was going on here?

On the fifth day of my hospitalization, I overheard the head nurse talking to someone who looked like he worked in administration about my room, "She is not supposed to be down there. There is no bathroom or shower; she has to share with the other male patients." This brought quite a few questions to my mind:

Are they trying to sweep me over to L (Psychiatric Ward) and under a carpet because I am a female patient and they don't have a bed for me?

Could this be why I was not admitted the night I came here from the other medical center?

Why did it take so long in the morning to figure out what they were going to do with me? Could it be because they made the mistake of discharging me in this physical condition in the first place, and they didn't want to admit it to my congressman? Or could it be that they knew I wouldn't have had a mishap in my chair if I had the chair that was originally ordered for me, and they didn't want to admit that to anyone as well? Would I be in the physical and emotional state that I was in at the time if I were getting adequate healthcare?

A couple of days later, I had my monthly, "Let's take x-rays because we have to make sure you're not falling apart" appointment. When the results came back, the prognosis was good – I wasn't falling apart after all, and I hadn't broken or dislodged anything in my "Angela freestyles down the carport and hits the curb" accident. However, I wasn't fusing. The doctor told me that with that kind of a fall, combined with the kind of bone growth I was exhibiting, and the slow healing process could be the reason for the lack of fusion. He carefully explained to me that it, "really could have been a lot worse. Continue to wear your brace, take it off at night when you go to sleep and when you do your exercises," he advised.

The doctor evaluated me once again and – hooray!! He wrote a prescription for pain medication and put it in my chart! He also filled out a prosthetics request for a permanent-issue ultra-lightweight wheelchair! This time, I was determined to hand-carry the request to my Disabled American Veteran service officer, who promised to make copies and submit them to the proper authorities.

Learning that the majority of my current problems were a direct result of the surgeries I had a couple of months earlier, I began keeping a journal filled with questions…

Was the bone used for the additional bone graft from my left hip or from the bone bank?

What were the conditions that made it necessary to fuse three levels, instead of the two levels originally planned? Were these conditions assessed before the surgery took place or was it really just an error?

Is it less complicated to perform reparative surgery on the shifted bone segment before the new bone growth sets the bone segment?

Why weren't the loose bone fragments removed? And who were the surgeons involved?

What conditions during the second surgery caused the injuries to my knees and chest?

The intermittent headaches that I had been having were similar in severity to the ones I had during the time of my cerebral spinal fluid leak, how could I be sure that the tear has completely healed?

One of the orthopedic doctors stated that the surgeons knew about the tear during the operations, not after it. If this is true, why didn't they repair the tear?

There had been some concern over the positioning of a screw in my back. If the surgeons noticed that the screw was too close to my spinal cord, why didn't they relocate it?

I'd been encouraged by many people to write everything down for my own recollection. What started as just a letter to my Congressman's office had now become more of a personal journal. Not only was it a collection of my personal medical horror stories, but I discovered that it had a therapeutic, calming effect value, as well.

All I had to do was get a look at my medical records; I was positive that all the answers to my questions were sitting in a folder somewhere. But they wouldn't allow me to review them, telling me that a rehab doctor would have to authorize it. What happened to my rights?

The next time I saw the doctor, I asked him about my spinal cord injury and about the tear in my thecal sac. Since my spinal cord's involved, I told him, I wanted to go to SCI. But there seemed to be something wrong with my memory, because I forgot to ask any of the questions that I had been collecting in my journal. I couldn't seem to get through any appointment without forgetting something; was I losing it mentally? Could my sleep deprivation cause memory lapses?

It was 4:56 a.m. and I was in so much pain that I couldn't sleep – again. I found myself face down in my pillow, not able to breathe, just praying for an end. I was on my stomach and wasn't able to turn to my side from that position. I asked for the pain medication that my ortho doctor ordered but the nurse said that I was on the rehab ward, and only a rehab doctor had the authority to order it – because they could not order it for pain patients. I didn't belong in that ward.

———————

Every day, I'd ask for pain medication, but every night they gave me only a sleeping pill. On my fourth night, I realized, the pill hadn't helped so what was the point of taking one at all? By now I was rambling because I was exhausted, and the pain was racking my body. I had nothing to do but to look at the clock. 2:10, 3:20, 3:59, 6:14, 7:20 … no sleep for me that night, and no pain meds either.

After five very long days, I was discharged from the VA hospital with a loaner wheelchair, but with no place to go.

By this time, my state disability had run out. I could not establish an increase in veterans' disability compensation because the doctors, I later discovered, had expunged all evidence of wrongdoing from my medical records. They also wrote operative reports to cover their asses that did not include the truth about what happened during my surgeries. The doctors and students had continued to deny any wrongdoing during the surgeries back in September. In the real world of the workman's compensation system, if an employee is injured on the job, there is a system of benefits provided to the injured worker while they are disabled due to their industrial injury. This does not exist in the veterans benefit system. When a claimant has been granted a rating for service-connected disability, normally the veteran receives retroactive payments back to the original date of the claim. But I never received retroactive payments, and what little money I had in the form of veteran's benefits was not enough to sustain myself for the prolonged claim adjudication period?

You're probably asking yourself, "Why didn't you sue?" Blame it on the Feres Doctrine. Since 1950, this legislation bars service members from suing the government for peacetime medical malpractice and wrongful death cases. Medical care in the military varies. Some give good reviews about their care and other reviews range from adequate or average to simply criminal. Until the military is held to the same standard as the rest of the medical community, we will continue to have victims like me feeling as if we're nothing but guinea pigs.

Unfortunately, all the months I spent going for treatment, surgery, appointments, etc. caused me to miss a substantial amount of work. A new management team took over the company while I was gone and I was informed that I had been terminated.

My employer sent a letter addressed to me at the hospital that stated if my physical condition "improved" I could reapply for an entry-level position. At one point, my supervisor informed me that it was the new management's decision to fire me and bring in their own people. After some time had passed, a friend from work asked if I would come back. I had worked from a wheelchair before so I was considering the offer. I dearly loved that job. But I never went back.

I was discharged from the VAMC on Thursday, December 23, 1993.

That year, 1993, was the worst year of my life and I was more than happy to see '94 come in. But wouldn't you know? The New Year started where the old one left off. My life was falling apart.

CHAPTER 5:
LOSING
EVERYTHING

In the early weeks of January, my life was routine – just going to and from the hospital for various therapies, tests and appointments made up most of my day. But wouldn't you know? I couldn't go two weeks without another injury to my spine. While being transported to the VA Hospital, the tie-downs that strap the wheelchair in place in the transport van came loose and I was flipped over backwards. Once at the VA, the orthopedic doctor ordered X-rays that clearly showed that the bone graft had shifted this time and that it would be necessary for me to have more surgery. The orthopedic doctor ordered a spinal CAT scan that confirmed the orthopedics' recommendation. After a spinal myelogram, which uses a special dye to make X-rays clearer, I was given a consult to see a doctor in spinal cord injury.

My visit with the chief of Spinal Cord Injury services wasn't very encouraging. After reviewing the results of the myelogram, he suggested that all my problems may be "psychological" and asked me to describe one of my typical days. Every day was the same, I told him. This was my life in limboland: I didn't sleep well and I woke up every morning thinking that the left side of my head was going to spontaneously combust at any given moment. If I turned over I experienced agonizing pain in my back so I almost never wanted to move or even try to get out of bed. When I did finally get up, I tried to avoid the growing pile of undone laundry that awaited me. I would get dressed and go to the kitchen to make myself coffee trying to steer clear of the unpacked boxes and dirty, days-old dishes that also awaited me. By the time I was done with all of that, it was usually 11 am, and time to go outside and wait for the taxi that came to take me to the VA three days a week for my personal care. Everyday, I left thinking maybe I would get better, but every time, I got back home, knowing that I would not. Then I try to fix myself something to eat and later, I write or lie down and watch TV. Every night I went to bed just hoping and praying that I wouldn't wake up the following day and that if I do, that it would be a better day than the day before. All of my yesterdays were the same. And I always hoped that my tomorrows would be different.

The Chief of Spinal Cord Injury stood and looked at me. Instead of sympathy, understanding or any kind of support, he simply stated that I was "a waste of human life." I was so discouraged, I could do nothing but cry... then I got angry. I was angry at the doctors, my situation, and the ridiculousness and the seemingly hopelessness of it all. My life was falling apart and it was just getting worse. When I returned home that day an official note from the sheriff's office was tacked to the front door of the apartment that I had shared with my partner stating that an officer would be there the following day to evict me. After all of my months of rehabilitation and recent hospitalization, I came home to discover that she hadn't paid the rent – or the utilities. When I opened the door to the apartment, it was a mess; practically everything I owned was gone and the utilities were shut off.

All that was left were a few pieces of furniture and my personal items, my clothes, her dog, Shiloh, and the stacks of unpaid bills and unpaid car payments for the car on which I had innocently and trustingly co-signed for her.

Numb in my wheelchair, I couldn't really comprehend what had happened; it was all too surreal. I felt shocked, outraged, overwhelmed, stunned, and traumatized. As I tried to understand the enormity of it all, my partner of 4 years who had abandoned me walked in. She was unaware that I had been discharged; she was more than surprised when she saw me in the middle of the living room. All she could say was, "I did not sign on to be with someone in a wheelchair." It left me sick and empty inside. She then took the car, "Why not?" she said, "You're never going to drive again." And then she drove off leaving behind her dog, Shiloh. That was the last time I saw her.

Later, I learned that she had also stolen my final state disability checks, wiped out all of my savings, and stole my 401K check from my former employer. She had deposited everything in our joint checking account and then promptly removed it all. I was completely cleaned out. I had lost everything.

After my eviction, I moved what little I had left into a locker at Disneyland, just outside the front entrance on Harbor Boulevard in Anaheim. With nowhere to go, Shiloh and I lived on the streets. For a week, I slept upright in my wheelchair by the bus bench near Disneyland but realized that I had to move on. Then I began hanging out at the VA and met with a representative from the Disabled American Veterans (DAV), DAV assisted me in finding temporary housing near the Veterans hospital where I was receiving my personal care.

It really sucked at the time but looking back on it, I guess you could say that it all worked out for the best. Shiloh kept me safe on the streets and would become my trained service dog. I got the better end of that deal as Shiloh was a much more loyal and worthy companion. I discovered that I didn't need all of the material things that I had collected through my life and without having to answer to the demands of a "normal" life, I could adjust better to life in a wheelchair.

My headaches continued all through spring and, once again, I was bounced from Spinal Cord Injury (SCI) to Neurology and the ER for treatments or diagnoses. Finally, I was admitted to SCI in late April. However, after a week of bed-rest, IV fluids, robaxin (a muscle relaxant) and vistaril (an antihistamine used to treat anxiety), the doctors could see no improvement in my condition. I was discharged.

The new apartment that I shared with the DVA representative was difficult to get into and out of. It was too difficult to do the laundry, so I gave up trying. My bladder incontinence never improved, so I continued to wear pads, or if I ran out, anything I could get my hands on. I was totally on my own and failing miserably. SCI was not treating my back and dislodged bone grafts, and orthopedics seemed to have forgotten about me or had written me off. I felt powerless and unable to affect any sort of change in my life or the system that had been strangling me for years.

When I celebrated my thirty-fourth birthday on May 10, I found myself wishing I had never been born. My weight had ballooned up to 350 pounds, which made me feel more immobile than ever. I knew that I would never live the life that I had before, but if I could just get some of my medical problems resolved, maybe, I thought, just maybe I could have a life worth living.

———

I only received $87 a month from the Veterans Administration. State disability ran out, I was told I was ineligible for welfare and public assistance because I was a veteran who was eligible for veteran's benefits. Was homelessness my only option? I couldn't face living on the streets again. A combination of the slow adjudication process at the Veterans Administration, lack of documentation in my medical records, lengthy medical treatments, and lack of medical treatment are the key ingredients in the government's recipe to create a homeless veteran. I first filed my claim for benefits after my discharge from the USMC in 1981 and requested an increase, been denied, and re-appealed the decisions repeatedly. I was fighting a battle that no disabled veteran, no matter what the length of service or combat related status should ever have to fight. It certainly was not the one I was trained for.

I felt hopeless and helpless, lost and alone. If I had a gun nearby, I probably would have used it to kill myself.

CHAPTER 6:
KNOCKED DOWN
BUT NOT OUT

When June rolled around, I made the decision to travel to San Francisco to attend the Disabled American Veterans' state convention in the Bay Area with another veteran who was also a wheelchair user.

This was my first trip away from home. I was hesitant to go, but all of my friends encouraged me, "It will be good for you," and "You need to learn how to get out there sometime." I was just learning to become independent in a wheelchair but still defiant at the thought of having to depend on it and thought I could handle anything.

One night my wheelchair friend and I were in the underground BART station. It was dark and lonely with no one else around. As I pushed myself along looking for the elevator, I was totally unaware that I was moving closer and closer to the edge of the platform. The floor was shiny and I could see the ceiling lights reflecting off the tiles but couldn't quite see the edge. As I rolled forward, one of my front wheels got caught in a crack, and I was thrown headfirst onto the train tracks five feet below.

My friend's screams caught the attention of two passersby. These two good Samaritans jumped down on the tracks, managed to pick me up and place me on the platform just moments before the seventy-foot long, 56,000 pound BART train would have hit me. When I regained consciousness, I had difficulty breathing and was unable to move my arms and legs. I believed that I had just broken my neck.

Funny things go through your head when you believe you only have seconds of living left. I found myself thinking that I should have been more thankful for everything I had because, as I discovered, it can be much worse. I hadn't truly lost everything and I had plenty more to lose. Instead of anger over everything that had happened to me in the last couple of years: botched surgeries that left me a paraplegic, joblessness, and homelessness, I should have been more appreciative of the life I had left.

As I lay in San Francisco General Hospital with sixteen stitches and a mild brain injury that left me dyslexic with numbers, this injury, more than any of the others, sealed the deal and made it impossible for me to return to any career in the engineering field. It was also the pivotal point in my acceptance of disability.

Of all the hardships and disappointments that came crashing down on me, the accident in San Francisco changed my life more than any other. I started believing more in creating or being an active participant in my future and in the shaping my destiny. I slowly began accepting my physical condition. This accident inspired me to live life more fully than I had been. I stopped thinking and feeling as though I had lost everything and began creating a new life for myself.

I knew I couldn't go back to the mental state that I had been living in. My twenties and thirties were spent going to and from hospitals and medical appointments, living well below the poverty level and being unable to care for myself. I knew that I couldn't go on like that. Well, I guess I could have, but I had a choice – either resume the angry and pitiful life, described by the chief SCI doctor as a "waste of human life," or get up and get on with a new life and become a powerful force for change. I may have lost the use of my legs, and more than once, a home, but I hadn't lost my ability to use my able-bodied mind, opinions, thoughts and actions. From that moment on, I looked for opportunities to make a difference.

Ten days after my accident, I received a letter from the VAMC Prosthetics Department asking for me to return the loaner wheelchair: "Receipt for loan of U.S. Government Property," signed by the Chief of Prosthetics." Oh no, not him again! Why was the VA asking for me to return the wheelchair? I'd only been out of the hospital for a week, and now, they wanted it back? Of course, my previous experiences with the Chief of Prosthetics had proven that he'd made choices that have had an adverse effect on me, my medical treatment, and my physical well-being. The old Angela would have internalized the anger and just taken it but the new and improved Angela wanted to do more. I took charge, organized a protest at the Veteran's Hospital and notified the media.

The powers that be decided not to repossess my wheelchair pending a full medical exam. I had become quite the warrior in the struggle. I was determined not to take any more abuse!

———

I applied for vocational rehabilitation benefits; however, after all the testing and interviewing with various vocational education counselors, I was told that I failed all of the testing. Test results were no doubt affected by the traumatic brain injury in San Francisco. At this point I was just wondering what I should be doing with my life.

While receiving treatment at the VA, I met some veterans who spoke about the Veterans Wheelchair Games. Established in 1981, it is the largest wheelchair sports competition in the world with seventeen different sports for veterans who use wheelchairs due to spinal cord injuries, amputations or neurological diseases.

But even after much discussion with family, friends and doctors, I felt fearful. The accident in San Francisco was a good excuse not to go, but the doctor's ugly words, "waste of a human life" turned my fear into action. I had to move forward, to walk in faith and believe that my abilities as a natural athlete extended far beyond just the use of my legs. I came to realize that I was so busy being angry – with the doctors, the VA, the nurses, so-called advocates, and anyone else who stood in my way, that I couldn't see what I was supposed to be doing with my life. I needed to move on and use my gifts – my gifts of leadership, athleticism, organization, and dedication.

Once I decided to take control of my destiny, I harnessed the energy that I had buried deep inside me and pushed it out. Once I told the universe who was the boss, the universe took a back seat and I created a new reality for me to live in. The first thing I did was to become a member of the only congressionally chartered veteran's organization, the Paralyzed Veterans of America. For more than sixty-five years, the PVA has offered research, education programs and activities to the 750,000 people in the U.S. with spinal cord injuries and spinal cord diseases.

The year 1993 was a year of recovery; 1994 was a year of rehabilitation and I would have been damned if my future was going to be the same as my past. Despite being a novice, I signed up for the 1995 National Veterans Wheelchair Games and made the trek to Atlanta, Georgia. Since it was my first time attending the games, my flight and hotel expenses were fully sponsored by the California Paralyzed Veterans Association (CPVA).

For one glorious week in June, hundreds of wheelchair-bound athletes come together and display feats of hope and courage. A special "Kid's Day" program allowed children with disabilities to meet the athletes and be introduced to wheelchair sports.

Even though I didn't have the use of my legs, I still had a competitor's heart and spirit. Competing made me feel alive again! For five days I participated in the games and won three gold medals in swimming (the 100-meter freestyle, backstroke and breaststroke), a gold medal in the wheelchair slalom course and a gold medal in billiards. Striding atop the podium, I felt like a winner in more ways than one. I knew at that moment that nothing could hold me back, that despite the hardships and trauma I had experienced in the previous two years. I and I alone, held my future in my hands.

I joined a number of basketball teams and in 1996, I returned to the National Veteran's Wheelchair Games and won three gold medals in swimming again, a silver in the slalom and a gold medal in the shot put. For the next four years I pushed myself to be the best athlete in a wheelchair I could be given my situation and circumstance.

I received a significant increase in my disability compensation and the timing was good. I was able to purchase a home in 1997. My daughter's behavior hadn't changed. She had a baby, my first grandchild, and she would appear and disappear in my life randomly in the coming years just as she had in my past. I would help her financially whenever I could, I had to come to terms with the fact that our lives would never be like a sitcom where everyone's problems are resolved in thirty minutes. Just like having to come to terms with being disabled, I had to accept the fact that my daughter and I would never have the relationship that most mothers – and grandmothers – long for. So I put all my energies into continuing on with the life I had been rebuilding for myself.

Feeling confident in my athletic abilities, I was continually looking for new challenges to tackle. One day in 1998, my wheelchair basketball sponsor, who also ran an outdoor adventure program, needed an extra body for a "learn to row day." After some basic instructions, I was hooked; rowing came easy to me. Soon, I discovered adaptive rowing, which is specifically designed for rowers with physical or developmental challenges or disabilities. The adaptive boats are the same as able-bodied boats, but feature equipment that's adapted to accommodate persons with disabilities. The hull of an adaptive rowing boat is identical but is equipped with special seats, which offer 'postural support' for people who, because of spinal cord injuries like me, need their upper body kept in a fixed position. Plus, they're strapped into their seats for support while rowing.

I began evaluating, testing and designing adaptive equipment with the owner of Pacific West Rowing. He and his wife were extremely supportive of adaptive rowing and of me personally. I learned how to use my mechanical engineering background and problem solving skills to properly rig boats not only for regular adaptive rowers but also for elite fixed seat rowers.

In June, 1999, I traveled down the coast to San Diego to enter my first ocean rowing regatta – the five-mile Bay2Bay Race. Over 3,400 athletes from clubs, universities and colleges from across the United States attended. I'll never forget the rush I felt at my first rowing competition. I placed my scull in the water next to the dock; inserted one oar and extended the blade out and away from the dock, and locked the oar into the rigging. Then I fit the other oar into the rigging and locked it into place. I eased down onto the seat of the scull, placed my feet in the footings and tied the laces. I gently pushed away from the dock and headed north along Mission Bay. And just an hour and a half later, I came in first and won a gold medal for the twenty-two foot open row class. Initially there were only a couple of able body rowing entries and there was no class of disabled or adaptive. Over races of longer distances in the ocean it did not matter and I could do well against the able body entrants.

For the next few years, I participated in a number of regattas, continuing to win first place gold medals. I even reunited with one of my old time favorite sports – surfing. But it took me a while to get back out in the water. There was a time when I would put on a wetsuit, drove down to the beach, leaned my surfboard against the van and just sat and watched the surf, like I was going to go out. I did that for a few months before I actually mustered up the courage to get back out in the line-up. I still had "surf in a major surf contest" on my to do list. A few months later, I entered the U.S. Amateur Surfing Championship (ASP), for able-bodied people, and came in second in my class. Since it was an amateur surfing championship, I didn't take my desire to "surf in a major surf contest" off my list. But it was a step toward that goal. It was later, after being denied entry to a major surf contest in the USA that I found the Roxy Jam, or the Women's World Championships of Longboard Surfing, in Biarritz France. Some of my surfing friends informed me that the contest was open entry so I became a member of the ASP, Association of Surfing Professionals and entered the contest.

With my ASP membership, entry to the contest, travel and accommodations arranged, all that was left for me to do was to determine which board to take and to get some practice sessions using the board I would be surfing with in the contest. I had my 9'6" stealth Pope Bisect board which I had previously taken to Hawaii and had an awesome time. I purchased it specifically for traveling and at the time of purchase, Pope Bisect did not have a 10' board. So, I took my 9'6" to a few local spots and on the small wave days, it was a bit more challenging. (I usually ride a Harbour 10' San O epoxy surfboard.)

As the departure date drew nearer, I began checking the surf and weather forecast for Biarritz. The forecast was for small wave conditions and some rain. I have surfed Biarritz in two to three meter waves and was thinking the 9'6" would work; but after seeing the forecast and webcams I decided to call and inquire about the 10' Bisect board I had recently seen on the Pope website. The two-piece surfboard design is the easiest for me to travel with being differently-abled and requiring a wheelchair for ambulation. The case is approximately 5'x3'x8" and fits vertically on the footplate of my wheelchair. I place the carrying strap around my neck to keep it from falling forward. I place my duffle bag with cloths and what not on my wheelchair backrest like a backpack and can thus go wherever in the world I want to go to surf independently.

I called Karl Pope and arranged to meet him at the warehouse location in Santa Barbara. I told him what I was doing and what conditions I expected. We talked about surf history and the history of the Bisect. I found it all very interesting and probably could have stayed and chatted all day. I looked at all of the boards and found the one I liked. It was epoxy and quite light for a Bisect board. Though not as light as the carbon fiber hollow core stealth, it was similar enough to the 10' board I regularly surf so I decided to trade my old, shorter board for it. This took place the day before departure so I really had no time to surf it. I had my board and myself all packed up and ready to go all the time never knowing if they would allow me to participate in the contest. I was feeling anxious, yet trying to stay positive and hopeful (but not too hopeful), all the while remaining realistic in order to minimize disappointment and have a backup plan should they not allow me to participate (I always have a backup plan).

The flight was uneventful and I arrived in Biarritz on July 1. My baggage and surfboard, however, did not. Some really cool people offered me a ride to my hotel and I checked in with no problems. On the morning of the 2nd I took a cab to the contest site to see how far it was to my hotel and how to get there without getting lost. It cost me eight euros, not too bad. It was downhill most all the way there. It took about ten minutes to push in my chair or basically try and control and steer it blasting down the steep hill. I got to the venue and checked in without any problems. I was stoked! There was not the least bit of concern on their part about my entry and they were not going to turn me away. I pushed up the hill at least fifty minutes back to my hotel to find the airline had delivered my duffle bag. There was no sign of my surfboard. Many surfboards were lost and some never arrived. Simone Robb received hers about an hour prior to her first heat.

I had my board shorts and a couple of rash guards in with my clothing. I was hoping the water would not be too cold. Surf report indicated about sixty-five degrees Fahrenheit. My wetsuit was in the bag with the board. I got to the surf village and began inquiring about borrowing a surfboard. They had several soft boards for the volunteers that they allowed me to use. Ah... just to get in the water was wonderful. I did not care what board I had at that point. The waves were bigger than the days before the contest, but not as clean. There was a good rip going south. The temperature was more like 68, no need for the wetsuit. They had used plastic zip ties instead of a string to attach the leash to the board and it snapped on my second wave and I had to swim for it. Go back out? By the time I got all the way up the beach and the access ramp to see all of the foam boards with plastic zip ties, I said forget it and went back to my hotel.

I had my heat sheet and was to surf in heat two on the first day. The first heat was to begin at 11:00 AM. I got on the phone and called the airlines about my board and they still had not found it. I went to sleep that night having nightmares about foam boards and zip ties. In the morning, with still no sign of my board, I decided to go to the contest site early instead of waiting for a possible delivery. They directed me to look behind one of the tents for a board and all I found was this big yellow one. It was a 10' or 11', about five inches thick and looked more like a stand up paddle board than a surfboard. I took it out for a practice session, or I should say it took me. It paddled great going out. I might have chosen that board for the Huntington Longboard Crew Paddle around the pier on New Year's Day, but not for anything else. I could not get it to turn, which in certain conditions was okay, but the first day of the contest brought two to three foot waves in the afternoon at Bolsa Chica, with ten to fifteen knot onshore winds. The conditions that day could not have been any worse for my heat. I did not advance past the first round. That was never my plan, though. I was not there to compete against these women, the best women long boarders in the world. I went there to surf *with* them.

During the contest heat I had both a right and a left take-off, which were identical: Up to the knees, try to turn the board, catch the rail, end of story. I needed a 3.70 to advance. Screw trying to turn the board; on my next wave I was just going to try a parallel take-off to the wave, having the board turned more in the right direction and just go straight.

No wave came before the buzzer sounded and I was done. I took a wave in after the buzzer, going straight in the white water where I did a switch stance and a sit backwards ride. I was disappointed that I could not have done more. I spent the rest of the day watching the contest and socializing with some of the other surfers in Surfers Village. They served lunch every day and it was actually quite good. Evian and Fosters were the sponsors so there was plenty of free water and beer. Surfer's village was very accommodating with plenty of places to hang out. There was a VIP tent, a media tent and a couple of other tents just for the surfers. There was a changing area and an area for free massage treatments. There were a couple of free coffee vending machines to get espresso in the mornings, and there was big screen where you could watch surf videos, the actual surf contest or the band that was playing on stage. There was live entertainment every evening and it was all free. It was a very well organized event and the location was perfect.

The next day I went to the venue early and the conditions were small but the waves were clean. Simone Robb from South Africa pulled off not one but two 360's on one wave to advance. That was so cool! My surfboard was still on the missing list. I took Big Yellow out again early and had the same results. I twisted my left knee trying and ended up barely able to ambulate for the rest of the day. After applying ice all day to my knee I returned to my hotel room that night still completely lame. My hotel room was not wheelchair accessible and so I had to leave my chair out in the hall. I had not had to do the "butt scoot boogie" in a long time, but I did that night. I decided to talk to God: "I came here to do something and I have not yet done what it is that I came here to do so please, can I just finish?" Scooting around my hotel room on my butt I turned over on to my knees and kneeled as far as the pain would allow, then I bounced a bit on my knee and crunch, game on! I could surf on my knees again.

The third day of the contest was canceled due to poor conditions. I socialized with some of the surfers and rested my knee. I was being careful not to push it. The next day there were small, clean conditions, but still no sign of my surfboard.

I took Big Yellow out, being careful of my knee. The water felt great but I still could not surf like myself. The competition was getting closer and more exciting to watch. During the day, my board had been found and delivered to my room. When I got back to the room I began to inspect the bag that was torn in two places. I removed the board and assembled it making sure it was okay and no parts were lost or damaged. The board was fine. It was the fifth day of the contest. I took a cab because I thought screaming down the hills at thirty mph in the wheelchair with the surfboard might be a tad too dangerous. When I got to the beach conditions were small and clean again. Finally I had an opportunity to surf my board. I went out for a bit before the quarterfinals began.

––––––––––

It was time for the semi-finals and finals. The waves were slightly bigger and continued to increase in size throughout the day. I do not think they got bigger than one and a half meters, though. Still, clean with some pretty fun waves. Schuyler McFerran surfed the most consistently throughout the day. Between the semis and the finals they had an "expression session" and about twenty-five people signed up to surf in it. It was crowded, and with the tide the conditions were not very good, so I decided not to participate. After the finals, however, the tide changed, the crowds thinned and it was looking like a lot of fun. So, I went out into the water.

I surfed the best I had in a long time, in chest-to-head high sets. I was catching wave after wave. I had a beautiful ride that I took nearly all the way in to the rocks only to discover that most everyone in Surfer's Village was watching me. I was riding waves, doing switch stance, floaters and re-entry, cutbacks even a hang five! They were all cheering and carrying on. I had my own personal "expression session" and accomplished one of the things I had set out to do: increase disability awareness and education, changing the perception of what people think or know differently-abled people can do! The other surfers from the contest began popping up in the lineup and then I had done one of the other things I had set out to do. I had surfed with some of the best women long boarders on the planet. I had accomplished and done everything I had set out to do.

On Sunday, July 9, on the way down to the contest, the street looked like the end of the Tour de France. Shop owners were all waiting for me to wheel by and were cheering. They watched me fly down the hill and push back up the hill twice daily all week. I arrived at the venue for my pre-contest surf session. Simone was there early too. We went for a final surf together.

After that, I threw out my old, nasty been-in-the-water-everyday shoes, changed my clothes, packed up my surfboard and made ready to leave the contest site for the last time. After a tag-team competition some of the surfers and Linda Benson went out for a final surf session. It was my turn to sit on the wall in Surfer's Village and cheer as Linda took wave after wave, having what appeared to be a surf session similar to mine just the day before.

I got a ride with my board back to the hotel and the event organizers were kind enough to arrange and provide transportation for me to the airport in the morning. It was an excellent trip. Not perfect, but I got to do everything I wanted to do. My wheelchair held up for the entire trip (although the bearings finally disintegrated after I had connected to my final flight to LAX). I was treated with respect by the contest organizers and the other surfers. The flight back was uneventful and my luggage and surf-board were waiting for me at baggage claim. Check "Major Surf Contest" off the bucket list!

———————

Just as I finally became the master and commander of my own fate, the universe – remember the universe?—well, it reared its little head again and knocked me off course. There I was, forging a new life as an accomplished wheelchair athlete, excelling in basketball, surfing, rowing, and kayaking and then the "C" word snuck up on me—Cancer.

I began having pain in my chest wall and my left breast was getting bigger. Thinking that my pectoral muscles had increased from pushing the wheelchair I went to the VA just to inquire about a breast reduction. I went in for a mammogram and the doctor found seven tumors in my left breast, ductile hyperplasia and fibrocystic breast disease in both. I underwent one radiographic diagnostic test, and factoring in having a strong family history of breast cancer, a double mastectomy was suggested rather than undergoing long bouts of chemotherapy and radiation or other such efforts to save my breasts. I know what you may be asking yourself, "Why did you decide to have the VA hospital of all places take both of your breasts?" The answer is simple: I didn't have insurance to go anywhere else. Once I was accepted into the Spinal Cord Injury (SCI) clinic and I no longer had a claim pending, the quality of care I received changed.

But some things didn't change. The surgery went right but I was discharged to home care and was expected to look after myself. I don't know how they thought I could push a manual wheelchair after a radical double mastectomy, but I was forced to try. Big mistake; I got an infection and had to be hospitalized.

Once I got the all-clear from my doctors, I couldn't help but look forward to getting back on the water and return to competing. I had come so far in my abilities and attitude that I wasn't going to let something like a double mastectomy stop me. After the surgery, I went on to win the National Championship in Women's Adaptive Rowing in 2000.

Back home, I began asking why there wasn't a program or training facility in Long Beach. Pacific West Rowing provided all of my adaptive rowing equipment, but I had to drive an hour each way down to Dana Point. I wanted to row closer to where I lived.

While competing in the all-adaptive International Bayada Regatta in Philadelphia in September 2000, I couldn't stop thinking...why not? Since I couldn't find an adaptive rowing program in Long Beach, why couldn't I just start my own? I had no idea what I was getting myself into.

CHAPTER 7:
GETTING MY FEET WET

U pon returning home from Philadelphia, I approached the president of the Long Beach Rowing Association. When I suggested my plans, he was all for an adaptive training facility based in Long Beach, but concerned about how to even start a program like the one I proposed. So I volunteered to get it going. Pacific West Rowing sold me a boat with a fixed seat and pontoons (outriggers on each side which stabilize the boat), I bought some straps and other accessories, and the Long Beach Rowing Association donated some storage space. Occasionally, I'd spend my disability check on another boat or on more equipment. And with the help of a lawyer, I began the long, two-year process of applying for 501-C3 non-profit status. It was important to me that whatever shape or form the program took, it had to be a non-profit organization.

Then I had to plan out what I wanted the program to accomplish. Originally, I just wanted to row closer to where I lived, but soon, establishing the program took on a life of its own and I realized that there was a much bigger picture on which I wanted to focus. Of course, it had to be open to physically and developmentally challenged or disabled people, but I wanted to make sure that the program also provided instruction and training for competitive and recreational rowing. That meant hiring coaches. But believe it or not, as noble as the program sounded and as excited as I was, I couldn't find anyone who was interested. So even though I was a paraplegic who had never coached before, I took it on. The first order of business was attending the U.S. Rowing Level 1 coaching classes; I felt such a sense of pride when I received certification as a rowing coach.

Getting people interested in participating was the next step. First, I invited my friends from the VA hospital to come out and try rowing, and then I handed out flyers at local hospitals and rehabilitation centers. What started out as simply wanting to get closer to my beloved sport turned into the California Adaptive Rowing Programs, or CARP. By the end of 2000, I had thirty CARP members.

Yep, it sure seemed like the universe was working with me for a change and the dark cloud that seemed to hover and rain down on top of my head had disappeared. Was all the physical and mental drama of the previous twenty years finally behind me? I continued to achieve success with medals in basketball, rowing, and surfing, but kept expecting something – anything – to jump in my way…but it didn't. And I've never looked back.

Rising up, taking control of my life and forging forward definitely worked for me – so what was next? Competing on an international level, I set my sights on the World Rowing Championships, an annual week-long event that began in 1964. In 2002, FISA (French for "Fédération Internationale des Sociétés d'Aviron"), the International Federation of Rowing, which sets the sport's rules and regulations, sanctioned adaptive rowing events so the WRC was the next logical step for me.

It was the first year that adaptive rowing was included at the World Championships. Not only was I on the national committee to develop the Paralympics Program for Adaptive Rowing, I was also on the national team. In the beginning, we received no support from U.S. Rowing and we were financially responsible for our own training, travel and accommodations, so we managed our own individual fundraising. U.S. Rowing did, however, pay to ship our adaptive boats and equipment with the able-bodied athletes' boats.

Seville, Spain, 2002. It was the 25th World Rowing Championship and I was all signed up and ready to go on September 15. There were only a handful of women in the sport back then and I found myself competing against the men. On September 22, I finished my first international rowing event by winning a silver medal. Since then, I've become a four-time gold medalist – Milan, Italy in 2003; Banyoles, Spain in 2004; Gifu, Japan, 2005 and Eton, England in 2006.

My rowing world championship medals

International competition was, and continues to be, exhilarating, calming, positive, and meaningful. My Olympic dream became my Paralympic dream; I was on track and my "to do" list was getting shorter and shorter.

Well, all right! I felt I had mastered everything that I had set out to do. What could I sink my long oars into next? How about a row across the Atlantic Ocean!

I know what you're probably thinking, "Are you out of your mind? Why would you want to row across an ocean?" Because every week of training and working towards the starting line and wondering about the finish line places me closer to figuring out whom I am. Being alone or with a small crew in a boat with no motor, no sail and miles of sky and water puts a person in a continual state of self-discovery. And then, of course, is the challenge itself always calling out to me. After all, more people have climbed Mount Everest than rowed across the Ocean, but my decision didn't have anything to do with the mere fact that I would be the first disabled female to do it. In fact, I still would have felt compelled to row the Atlantic even if I were the seventy-fifth.

I knew that such a huge undertaking would mean coming face to face with my disability and physical limitations but I had a goal and a dream. Hard work, pain, and purpose will drive anyone to accomplish what they set out to do, right? So how was I any different?

You may think that rowing thousands of empty miles across the ocean would be the most difficult thing I'd ever done in my life. But how could it be any worse than the hospitalizations, the surgeries, and the constant pain that I lived with everyday? The fact that my spinal cord injury would require some additional equipment and possibly even assistance at sea for 60 days is only the half of it. Any rowing partner I teamed up with may have to fill in as my personal caregiver as well. But none of these concerns slowed me down and I put the word out that I was looking to participate in an open ocean rowing event.

Knowing that I was crazy enough to be interested, my friends forwarded an email from someone who was putting together an entirely disabled crew to participate in an international race. That "someone" was Jo Le Guen. Famous for helping to draw attention to the problem of ocean pollution through his organization, Keep It Blue, Jo had attempted to row solo across the South Pacific from New Zealand to Cape Horn, Chile in February, 2000. But after two months and only one-third into the 5,600-mile journey, he developed gangrene and was forced to quit; he was later rescued and flown to his native France where he had to have his toes amputated. Now he wanted to row across the Atlantic from New York to England in June, 2006 with a differently-abled crew. Even though he was looking for a male amputee, I immediately emailed him anyway.

We e-mailed back and forth for a week or so and I learned that he already had one member of the crew on board – another Frenchman named Franck Festor, who, in 1987, lost his leg after a motorcycle accident. After checking out all my accomplishments, Jo and Franck came to Long Beach in April 2005 to see if I "could do the job." After a few days of watching me row and surf, they were both convinced and I became a member of the four-man crew we called "The Differents?" The question mark was added to say that for all of our differences we have a lot in common with everybody else. Just because we are differently-abled, we are not so different and we can accomplish much more than what society says or thinks we can.

The three of us accomplished quite a bit during their visit – we decided on team uniforms and rowing clothing, as well as the selection of our solar, electrical and water desalinization and purification systems to outfit the boat, which arrived that August. We also met with a videographer about filming a documentary chronicling our training and race preparations. But we still had one more seat to fill before we could begin planning and training.

In addition to finding a fourth teammate, we needed sponsors. Our crossing was never to be used (as some feared) as a platform to speak out against the environmental issues that were so close to Jo's heart. In 1999, Keep It Blue lead protests against the oil company Total when one of its supertankers broke completely in two and spewed more than 10,000 tons of oil along the French coastline. Even though it had been over five years since Jo's involvement, we kept a low profile as we looked for backing.

In preparation for the journey, I began working with my doctor at the VA Hospital in hopes of trying to minimize the amount of medication and equipment I needed to bring. Even though my partners were amputees, I didn't know how familiar they were with my level of injury and my requirements. Since I wasn't able to bring a 60-day supply of catheters and personal care items with me, I had to find a way to sanitize and reuse the ones I had plus find a way to take care of my personal needs without the usual supplies. Some of the greatest risks for me were going to be pressure sores and urinary tract infections.

The VA made special braces for my feet. My first pair was a solid, thin plastic, non-articulating foot orthotic. They worked well for standing in a standing frame but there was too much pressure on them in the boat for rowing. Somehow, I broke them at the ankle right where a hinge would be. My second pair had metal hinges and moved at the ankle. Made with titanium and carbon fiber materials, they were designed to be as light and strong as possible and were able to lock and unlock. Even though I wore the braces constantly to make sure I wouldn't get any pressure sores from the braces, it was difficult to duplicate the environment and situation of usage. We would be rowing for two hours and resting two hours every day until we reached the finish line 2,500 nautical miles across the North Atlantic.

Part of preparing for any sort of sport no matter if it's baseball, basketball or skiing, an athlete needs to practice. Rowing is no different. In July, Franck, Jo, our newest member, and I traveled to Torquay, England to race. The weather conditions were rough but Franck and I worked together enough to know that we made a good team. After just a few nautical miles, we established a new record in our boat category, breaking the record by three minutes.

Now, I don't know what it is about guys but something happens when they get together. Before the new rower came into the picture, it was "Eat, Sleep, and Row!" once he came on board, everything changed. He did nothing but talk about sex and his anatomy. Ugh! It only takes one to start it. Soon, that's all they talked about. They didn't know how to talk about anything else. Don't think I'm a prude; I grew up with four brothers and I was in the Marine Corps, so I'm accustomed to this dynamic. But there was no way I could listen to that twenty-four hours a day, seven days a week for up to two months at sea! Eat, Sleep, Row, the sex talk has got to go… all I wanted to do is row!

As we continued to train we soon realized that new rower wasn't physically able enough to join "The Differents?" after considering everything he was asked to leave. Unfortunately, he didn't leave gracefully; in fact, he lashed out by trying to discredit us and our motivations. Back to square one with only three crew members. Then Frank contacted Pierre Denis, an amputee from Belgium whom he had met while participating in a running marathon event. Pierre was a well-mannered man, very kind and respectful and would get embarrassed when the other men talked about sex. From time to time, I would ask Pierre what Franck and Jo were talking about but he told me it was better that I didn't know. I think he asked them to tone it down because it bothered him. It once again became "eat, row, and sleep." Excellent! Now I can row.

Differents crew *(left to right):*
Pierre Denis, Franck Festor, Jo Le Guen and Angela Madsen

The signage, with Differents crew member names, on our four-person boat

Pierre Denis, Franck Festor, Jo Le Guen and I trained together for a year. With our particular handicaps, the preparations took on significant meaning because our needs were so very different than the average rower. We had planned, prepared, plotted; we were organized, primed, and pumped!

We traveled to La Gomera in the Canary Islands for the start of the 2005 race. We were all together at the Airport when Jo told us that he had an announcement. We found a quiet little place in the airport and he delivered the bad news. His whistle blowing against the Total Oil company's spill in '99 had come back to bite him in the ass and our project was the sacrificial lamb. Evidently, he had made some enemies who did not want to see him succeed. There were individuals, he explained, who were afraid that Jo would use the race as an excuse to invite media attention to the many lawsuits that the company had been fighting in court. We never intended to use our crossing as a platform to speak against anyone. They feared us, so they stopped us!

Unfortunately, in France, just an accusation of any financial impropriety will place anyone in a position of examination by the Ministry of Finance. Jo was not permitted to be a part of any organization or project; nor was he permitted to receive money while he was under examination. The two remaining sponsors we needed to get to the starting line and the relationship of project leader and any hope of getting to the start line were gone. Later, after an investigation, the charges were determined to be false and Jo was later cleared of all charges.

We trained hard all year, spent a lot of money and time attempting to achieve a goal, trying to live a dream only to have it killed off by politics. At the time it was devastating to our spirits, but later we viewed their actions as just another obstacle or challenge to overcome. I didn't care about issues or platforms, politics or revenge; I just wanted to row across an ocean. Failing to get to the starting line after all of the work and commitment was like dying an emotional death. Rather than abandon the idea of rowing in 2006, I set my sights on the Atlantic Rowing Race in 2007. A 2,500 nautical mile journey from La Gomera, Canary Islands on the other side to the Atlantic to Antigua, West Indies, and the race would be more than challenging even for someone physically and psychologically fit. No doubt, I felt like I could do it. I e-mailed Jo about doing the race solo and he suggested that I row with Franck; I liked the idea and so did Franck.

So we weren't dead in the water after all. We just did what we always did. Adapt, revise, rise up and find a new way to accomplish our goals and Go On!

After Jo and Pierre gave us their blessing, Franck and I officially entered to row the Atlantic Crossing 2007 – billed as the "World's Toughest Rowing Race."

CHAPTER 8:
PLANS TO ROW
THE ATLANTIC

I t was now the end of September 2006 with only 450 days until the start of the Atlantic Rowing Race. Believe it or not, that's not a lot of time. But the training for the 2006 race was a great dress rehearsal and we knew what we had to do and what it took to get it done.

Franck and I agreed not to use the previous name of Differents? on this new venture. If we were associated with Jo Le Guen in any way his enemies may have tried to shut us down again. To be extra cautious, we decided not to base the project and fundraising solely in France as we had the previous year. We even thought twice about asking Jo to serve as an advisor.

Because promises of sponsorships we received for our 2006 trip fell through, we decided to build a website seeking donations. After crunching the numbers, we determined that the total budget for the trip would be $150,000. You may be asking yourself, "$150,000…for a rowboat?" At first glance, today's rowboat may look like the same vessel ancient mariners used, but for ocean travel, in the 21st century, it's a pretty good idea to have a sea-worthy boat made of fiberglass. They're usually built from a kit, but really good used boats are a less expensive option. Then there's the much-needed equipment such as fixtures and fittings, hatches, oars, seats and rails.

Electronic equipment is a number one priority for any voyage including solar panels, wind generator, GPS, and VHF radio. Communication equipment such as satellite phones and transponders are another necessity. Add in safety equipment like life rafts, life jackets, and a watermaker, cooker, food, supplements plus plenty of sunblock, and insurance and you can see how expensive a simple row across the pond can be.

Our first task was to come up with the initial installment for the $2,500 entry fee by October 1. Next, we had to get a boat. Jo Le Guen suggested the boat he used in his 1997 voyage, then named the Atlantic Challenge. After Jo made his successful crossing he sold it to two amputees from Corsica who then made the crossing in 2005. Because of the previous relationship and friendship between Jo, Franck and the Corsica guys, they would allow us to make payments on the boat when no one else would. Since it had already been rowed across two times and was once owned by Jo, we thought the boat was fully equipped with all the necessary rowing, safety, and electronic equipment that we required. Franck handled all negotiations and dealt with purchase of the boat. We christened it "Rowoflife."

The boat has an interesting history in that it was built from a kit by prisoners in a French prison. Jo reasoned that rowing across an ocean was much like being incarcerated and that prisoners could be rehabilitated through ocean rowing. He had a prisoner released to row with him. That prisoner was incarcerated for double murder and earned his freedom by rowing across the Atlantic. Rehabilitated, he has never been in trouble since! I met him at one of our training sessions in France. Seemed like a nice enough guy but must admit… the wielding of the steak knife at the dinner table did make me feel a little nervous.

After we paid the entry fee and the purchase details of the boat were arranged, we felt like we were off to a great start—but there was still so much more we needed. I had very little experience organizing fundraisers and looking for sponsors (I'm just a rowing coach and an athlete; after all), I picked up the phone, made the calls and put out the word. Ideally, we should have been concentrating our efforts on training and preparation but Franck and I both knew that if we wanted to compete in the 2007 Atlantic Rowing Race, we had to work on every aspect of the project together. What's the old saying, "If you want your dreams to come true, you better not sleep?" Well, Franck and I worked twenty-five hours a day, eight days a week to realize our dream.

It was vitally important to both of us that we dedicate our race to the cause of human rights and about accepting people regardless of differences—echoes of The Differents? to be sure, but it's the heart and soul of our lives and certainly of this competition. As I've mentioned before, rowing is mostly solitary and a person spends a lot of time alone in close quarters with perpetual personal enlightenment, but it doesn't take a rocket scientist to know that basic human rights and respect are denied to a great many people. My personal experience and some of the reasons I feel I get no respect is because 1) I'm a woman, 2) I'm a lesbian and 3) I'm a paraplegic.

I believed then, as much as I do today, that everything would fall into its place in the world if people could just learn what human rights are and practically and non-discriminately apply them to their lives. Human rights must be respected for all human beings regardless of race, color, religion, gender, age, orientation, social status, income level, etc. I don't believe a person can stand up for human rights and still harbor emotions or violence against any one individual or group of people for any reason. We are all equal partners in life. We all share in the responsibilities of protecting our planet, our children, our freedom, and each other. Through awareness and education we really can change the world! When human rights become a fact, peace will be a reality!

In-between all the phone calls, emails, web building, and fundraising, I knew I had to begin a steady dose of hard core training. The first step in training was the gym at the Sea Beach Naval Weapons Station and the Long Beach Rowing Association. After putting a schedule together, I jumped on the indoor rowing machine, began strength training and started a cardiovascular program. I also put in a request for a hand cycle. I began working out continuously: a couple of hours in the morning and a return trip in the evening to work with a trainer for an additional two hours. But in January 2007, I was informed that the trainer was no longer permitted to work with me because she wasn't certified to train people with disabilities. I was told that I could still use the gym, but that I would have to do it on my own. Well, at least they didn't boot me out the door.

I continued my steady state training, which is slow and continuous training for endurance, on the indoor rowing machine. In-between my gym workouts, I put in two hours of rowing per day. Not only did I have the Atlantic race on my mind, but I had a long to-do list of competitions that I was preparing to attend in the next few months. Women's World Longboard surfing championships in Biarritz, France; Veterans Wheelchair Games in Milwaukee, Wisconsin; Rowing Nationals in Princeton, NJ; National Rowing Team Training camp in Philadelphia; and the World Championships of Rowing in Munich Germany. I also had to finish up a course in celestial navigation and obtain a marine radio operator permit.

By this time, my daughter had been diagnosed as being bipolar and became an insulin-dependent diabetic; she also suffered other health problems. No wonder she was difficult as a child. During this time she got married and had two more daughters. It is not easy being a parent of a bipolar child, nor is it easy for my granddaughters having a bi polar parent or my son-in-law having a bi polar spouse. I still believe all of the hardships my military service and disability generated played a role in some of her condition responses and her behavior but I do understand the role of mental illness and her behavior much better now. When she came to back into my life and explained to me that she had been diagnosed bi-polar it made complete sense to me. Yep, that explains a lot.

After all the training, the websites, the phone calls and all the hard work trying to find money, sponsors and investors, Franck and I were discouraged when our requests for sponsorship and support were turned down and rejected by nearly everyone including my gay and lesbian groups, my veterans groups, spinal cord injury groups, amputee organizations and numerous other general organizations and corporations. This, and the lack of media response and interest, was a shocking disappointment to us. When I spoke to people about the problems we were having getting support and sponsors for our project, people were astonished. But we both kept getting rejection after rejection. I don't know if I would have gotten more support for a solo row or not but I was not going to abandon Franck to find out. It was as though the only ones who believed in us were our family, our friends and people that actually got to meet us and speak with us about our project. But nothing was going to stop us. We believed in ourselves, our mission, and wholeheartedly believed that we could get us where we needed to go!

CHAPTER 9:
PREP, PREP AND MORE PREP

With all of my accomplishments, medals and citations in surfing, the wheelchair games and adaptive rowing, you would think that my being physically challenged wouldn't be an issue in trying to raise funds and find sponsors for our Atlantic crossing. But there were (and still are) just way too many who think people with disabilities aren't capable of anything except breathing and occupying space on a couch. This seemed like an excellent reason to row across an ocean!

Franck didn't seem to be having any trouble in France but it just seemed as though I had to go through more difficulties than anyone in trying to make the Atlantic Race happen. I didn't know if it was my disabilities, my gender or what the problem was. Was it because the French are more supportive of the disabled? Or could it have had anything to do with the fact that he's a *male* amputee? The one thing I did know was that we only had 315 days until the start of the Atlantic Race in the Canary Islands and he was the only one getting any kind of support – he even managed to get the support of the French Foreign Army. But I couldn't get any support for our project here in the U.S. at all. I was happy we were getting some kind of acknowledgement from someplace, but I couldn't help but be a bit envious when Franck was so excited about the support he was receiving. I am competitive and don't want to be outdone, not in sports or even in support.

However, we did have one thing in common in our fundraising efforts – we each seemed to have the same problems garnering support from the disabled sporting associations and publications. We had each written and submitted articles about our endeavor to a number of magazines and had each been rejected. For the life of me I couldn't understand what the issue or problem was. We were both getting frustrated and we both felt that we were two alone without a country. Were organizations withholding support because of our nationalities? Nah, that couldn't have anything to do with it. Who in America could possibly care that I was rowing with a Frenchman? And who in France could care if a Frenchman was rowing with an American? For God's sake, it's the 21st century; no one could possibly harbor Franco-American resentment of any kind.

Besides, we both planned to represent our countries and the human race in everything we wanted to do and the issues we wanted to address in our crossing had no boundaries and were global. So why did we get little or no support from our disabled communities, from the human rights organizations, from environmental groups? On top of everything else, I was pretty astonished when I didn't get support from the gay and lesbian community. I never thought that group, of all people, would discriminate against anyone, let alone the disabled.

The bottom line was (and still remains) that ALL the groups treat their disabled poorly. Hell, even the disabled community was a shocking disappointment. Perhaps they didn't want us to set and achieve such an ambitious goal. But Franck and I weren't trying to send any kind of, "if we can do it, you have to do it" message. Two disabled athletes crossing an ocean doesn't mean that every disabled person has to do it. I don't feel like I have to do a summersault off a vertical ramp in my wheelchair just because someone else did it (although that may be a safer and much easier thing to do than to row across an ocean). Quite a few people climb Mt. Everest, too, but does that mean the entire population will be required to do it? I don't think so.

Initially, I was hoping to utilize my share of the ad space on the boat for U.S. sponsors like the Surfrider Foundation, Green Peace or some alternative energy and environmentally conscious organizations. But for reasons I still can't explain, they weren't interested. Neither were military groups, veterans groups, disabled veterans, or organizations in the disabled community. We were Ocean Rowing's Spanky and his friends from the *Our Gang* film series of the 1930s. I think it's funny and prophetic that one of my favorite episodes was the soapbox derby where the kids whose parents had money also had the best race cars and the kids from Spanky and the gang had to use junkyard stuff to build their racer (and if I remember correctly, Spanky won the race). That just shows what I've always felt – it's not our physical disabilities that make us underdogs or challenges us nearly as much as what we have to work with.

Even with no financial support on the horizon, Franck and I planned to meet in France on March 24 for two weeks worth of training so I had a lot of prep work to do. Even though I lost my trainer earlier in January, I continued to train at the gym on base on my own for five days per week up to four hours at a time. My training made me stronger every day but my orthopedist warned me that I had only 50% of the lateral meniscus left in one of my knees and that it could be arthritic and, oh yeah, in case I forgot, he reminded me that I was also a paraplegic. And, of course, there's always the "you're not as young as you used to be" speech that most doctors give their patients: "Remember, Angela, you're forty-six, not twenty." At least he and my primary care doctor gave me the green light to go ahead with the crossing.

I became more optimistic when my local chapter of the Paralyzed Veterans of America agreed to sponsor us with a monthly stipend that would go towards the entry fee. It was only 1/5th of the monthly payment but it was something… and something was better than nothing. Plus, individual contributions of $5's, $10's and $20's were coming in as well as encouraging notes and cards. The universe was working with me once again.

I focused back on my training. Although I always prefer to get on the water and row, it wasn't always possible. Luckily, the gym had a Concept2 ergometer also known as a rowing machine. Concept2 is probably the world's best rower for off-the-water training. I'm sure you've seen one –

the most common has a flywheel connected to a chain and handle. Normally, once you're seated, you place your feet in the foot straps and push your body backwards with your legs, then pivot your back and pull on the handle, causing the flywheel to spin. The flywheel's mechanism simulates the feel and resistance of an oar rowing though the water. Rowing is great exercise even if you're not prepping for an international race; it burns way more calories than a bike or hand crank and is a total body workout even for those with disability. There is no overhead shoulder rotation and no impact on the body. The benefit of static load bearing for Paras and Quads in rowing is phenomenal.

When mid-March arrived, I was mentally and physically prepared to meet up with Franck, but then came the news that the boat wasn't ready and the training trip had to be postponed…that's okay, I thought; the delay meant more time to work out so I intensified my training at the gym and focused on an aggressive five-day simulated training session.

I just needed to rev up my training, stick to a schedule, put in the time, and do the work. My goal was to get to the point past physical and mental discomfort and get into the "the zone." In order to truly simulate the sixty-plus days I'd be at sea, I needed to eat, drink and sleep the two hour schedule of work and rest. My training began on a Monday at 7:00 in the morning. Although distractions such as the TV, computer and telephone could sometimes play havoc with my simulated training schedule, I averaged between 9,000 and 10,000 meters per session (about six miles), rowing two hours on and resting two hours taking a sixty-second water break every fourteen minutes while rowing. One two hour work session per day was spent at the gym lifting and one two hour session was spent on the water rowing in a boat. I never experienced muscle soreness or cramping but I knew from past training that I needed one-and-a-half gallons of water for every twelve hours of rowing or else I'd feel the pain.

By Thursday morning, during the 10:00 am rest shift, I had the first break-thru sleep. I woke up less than two hours later feeling rested and ready to go another two hours. Sleep and work was consistent for the next four rest periods so I had accomplished what I felt I needed to do. In less than five days, I rowed thirty-two, two-hour shifts for a total of 289,000 meters (179 miles) and I lost a total of sixteen pounds—all on a little ol' Concept2 rowing machine. My friends called it the "Insane Train."

My braces caused sores on my legs and feet, and blisters covered my hands. I should have used my leather golf gloves; in the past, they've reduced the severity of blisters but didn't entirely prevent them. Golf gloves are also thin enough to operate the GPS system without removing them and they also tend to grip better when they're wet.

Not only was I training my body, but I was also evaluating the various products like seat cushions and energy bars we'd be using on our two-month voyage. While at sea, I knew that I'd need to take in a minimum of 5,000 calories a day – a diet of canned tuna fish, Luna Bars, omega-3 peanut butter and whey protein shakes made with water are the standard diet staples.

My training had taken my full attention and by the time I realized that my CARP classes were in jeopardy, it was almost too late. As I've mentioned before, I coach and teach rowing to other disabled people through the California Adaptive Rowing Program I established in 2000. It's not that difficult to organize and teach, but I couldn't seem to find anyone interested in taking over for me. Through the years, I'd go to Cal State Long Beach and do public speaking and presentations on behalf of my program. The teachers offered the students extra credit to volunteer but that usually turned out to be a one-time commitment. Sometimes a student or two would continue to volunteer, but none would take an interest in full time teaching. I needed people who not only wanted to learn to teach but to coach the sport as well. When I began, I didn't know how to teach…I barely knew how to row so I know for a fact that just about anyone can do this job! More than anything else, it requires patience.

With all of my rowing commitments piling up, only having 197 days and counting to find a replacement; come mid-June, I'd have to train someone or make the decision to cancel the program. I'd be away every other month and then I'd be participating with Franck in the Atlantic Race from November 2007 until February 2008. I absolutely hated to think the kids would not be able to row in my absence, but one of our rowers who stopped rowing due to shoulder pain decided to step up to the plate and help out. She did a great job when she started out, but when I got busy with travel and left her unsupervised, I later discovered that my rowing program and my finances were in trouble. It was before online banking and I once again found myself in a position of having to trust someone else with access to my finances; although this time it was under a totally different set of circumstances, the results were the same. I counted the $30,000 in losses over the time as the additional costs of pursuing a dream.

While my training was something I could definitely control, my finances were beyond my grasp. So far, our biggest sponsor was my local chapter of the Paralyzed Veterans of America who purchased a pair of oars. It wasn't much and we still needed $2,100 to make one of the monthly payments. Even with budgeting and cutting back I still didn't think we could make it. I had to sell some surfboards, rent out a room in my house, then I had to make a decision that gripped my heart – I came to the realization that I could no longer afford to support my disabled daughter, my three granddaughters and my son-in-law. I had to stop enabling them and had to learn how to look after my own interests before anyone else's.

I also had to commit financially to my rowing competition schedule, which included the World Championships in Munich in August. In order to be able to compete at the 2008 Paralympics in Beijing my national team rowing partner and I would have to qualify and be within the top eight finishers in Munich. We did not medal in Munich but we were fourth after the World Championships. My plan was to fly to Germany, meet up with Franck and get some on-the-water training with our boat, *Rowoflife*. I was really looking forward to the two of us just rowing; no cars, no hotels, no airplanes. It's really sad when rowing a 1,200-pound boat nonstop for three weeks is like a vacation, but it is a true testament to the degree of difficulty and stress people with disabilities face just to leave their house everyday. The rowing part is easy!

CHAPTER 10:
TRAINING IN
FRANCE

Unfortunately, Franck couldn't get the time off of work to meet me in Munich for the World Championship in August. So at the end of July, I flew to Europe and met up with him near the border of Spain in Biarritz, France, where I was surfing at the Roxy Jam Women's World Championships of Longboard Surfing.

Posing in front of *Rowoflife* in Biarritz, France

Then we promptly headed north to Lampaul, the home of Jo Le Guen. The three of us hadn't seen each other for over a year so our meeting was bittersweet; after a few rounds of "if only The Differents? could have competed in 2006," Franck and I eagerly made plans for our first training row.

However, the first two days together were not spent training like I had hoped but, instead, the two of us met with various media and potential sponsors. Later, when I finally saw our boat, I was bitterly disappointed. It looked exactly the same as when I'd seen it almost a year earlier. There was nothing new about it and no repairs had been made. It had no sponsors, no information, and its name hadn't even been painted on.

Trailered blank white silent boat without logos

Finally, after all the months of anticipating our first row with our new boat, we put *Rowoflife* into the water at the port of Lampaul, an exposed beach break that's famous for its great surfing. Franck and I headed south 230° towards the Stiff Point Lighthouse. It felt so great to know that our boat, with all its history, was now under our command. As we pointed our boat toward the Atlantic, it wasn't too long before I noticed that our seats needed to be replaced and the mounting holes had sheared and were rubbing against the mounting rails making them not only uncomfortable, but also unsafe.

The current was in a good condition but the wind was against us the entire way out. We made it to the lighthouse but as we began to head back the wind changed and we found ourselves struggling against the current. We continued to thrash against the powerful wind and attempted to take turns and row in shifts but one person could not row into the headwind and maintain enough speed to steer and hold a course with the rudder. Good thing Franck and I were so strong, it took our combined strengths to traverse the rocky coastline and take a safe course into the harbor. Later, when we showed Jo where we began our training, he firmly informed us that the area wasn't exactly the best and safest place to train. However, I was having, believe it or not, a great time. I feel most comfortable and exhilarated when I'm up against forces (almost) as strong as my own and I looked forward to the days of training ahead of us.

The next morning Franck and I headed out of Lampaul again, this time at a 260° heading. But once again, we headed straight into the wind. The current was not really a factor but the wind was so intense we couldn't row in shifts. We hit a cross tailwind on the way back to port and ended up about two miles north of the port's entrance, which meant that in order to safely cross the harbor entrance, we had to row back south and into the wind.

On day three of our training, we came head to head with the headwind once again but this time we rowed 250° to the south. This slight change allowed us to row about three to four miles more than the day before but on our row back to port, we came up against the same cross tailwind.

Still trying to figure out the best way to get around the wind, we set out the next day at 240°. Although we increased our distance and time, we were still unable to row in shifts due to the steady wind. Three straight days of wind, currents and rocky coastline made it impossible for us to train in shifts like we needed. Jo suggested that we take the boat to the Port of Brest, which is situated in a landlocked bay and better protected by the wind. "So, it's a great place to row?" I asked. "It would be interesting," he replied. Hmm, whatever could he mean?

It was raining when we set out to row south from Lampaul to the Port of Brest. Once again the wind was strong and head on. The current was south at about 1.5 knots and with us for the most part until we reached the point where we needed to turn. We tried to row in shifts but after turning in circles a couple of times we just accepted the fact that we would both have to row the entire time. Jo told us that the trip would take six or seven hours – but that was without a wind; it took twice as long as Jo estimated.

Conditions also changed as soon as we passed the Isle of Moléne, off the northwest coast of France, and once the island's protection ended, we were full on into the wind and waves.

The current stayed with us as we rowed with just enough speed to control the steering and direction of travel in relation to the waves. When we reached the point where we needed to turn we seemed to be in an eddy of current and the waves generated were fairly large. Jo failed to mention the nine to ten foot waves that seemed predetermined to hit us at the headland waypoint. It was then that I then realized that we were lacking some very important pieces of safety equipment – we were without a life raft, VHF radio, lights, and harnesses. We had little food, a few bottles of water, a handheld GPS and two life jackets. You might ask yourself how I could leave port without all the proper safety equipment. I didn't know at the time that the boat was as empty looking on the inside as it looked on the outside. Since Franck purchased the boat and it had made previous crossings, I assumed (I know "assume" makes an "ass out of u and me") that the boat was equipped with all the necessary safety gear. We needed to train, so I threw caution to the wind, so to speak, and headed out. It was a coastal row and Jo seemed to think we would be ok. What I know now is that rowing 800 miles at sea would be safer than near the rocky coastline off the north coast of France!

Talk about Mr. Toad's Wild Ride! The waves were fierce – at one point my GPS was reading three feet below sea level; then we listed up to the top of the wave and it read +18 feet. As wild as it was, it felt comforting;

waves always remind me of surfing so I couldn't help but think about some of my surf buddies back in California. I tried to talk Franck into rowing harder at one point to try and surf the boat, but the boat was too heavy and we rowed for hours after we had made the turn. I kept checking the GPS, thinking that it was malfunctioning or was just plain stuck but the truth was we weren't going very far in the wind and current. It felt like we were stationary – and, in fact, it took three hours to row 1.6 miles! After seven hours of rowing, we still had 10.5 miles to go just to get to the port entrance. Once we reached the port entrance, it was another few miles to the boat dock.

Even though the wind was still against us, we either somehow rowed out of the current or it had stopped because we finally began making progress. But it was still a constant struggle and we didn't know if we'd be able to make it to the port entrance before dark. The winds had doubled and we were caught up in a storm or gale. It was still light and since we had some visibility I tried looking at the GPS, landmasses and rocks to try and memorize our location. The French Army had an entrance to an area on our port side and our destination was also on the port side so even though we were two miles short of our last waypoint, so I instructed Franck to row into the French Army area. It took about an hour to get to the rock jetty.

We were rowing head on into gale force winds but once we reached the entrance and went inside the port, we had protection. I wanted to continue to row further into the safety of this inner harbor but Franck was worried about the Army area being off limits. His bright idea was to row two more miles against gale force winds and rain in the dark, after we had already rowed for more than twelve hours straight, taking very few breaks for food or water. He may not have understood my English, but my body language and tone of voice definitely let him know that I wasn't going to go along with his idea and just say "whatever." I insisted we keep going inside the harbor.

Then a sailboat, also looking for safe harbor, came to the entrance and I motioned to Frank that we should follow it. By now, the sun had completely set and it was so dark that it was impossible to see. Luckily, the sailboat had lights and it seemed to know where it was going; but Frank still refused to row and wound up calling Jo for help. Soon, the Army came out and gave us a tow into the harbor. Later, we tied off safe and sound fairly close to the sailboat I wanted to follow. If we had gone back out we could have possibly made it the two miles but then again maybe not.

We headed out the next day and once again the weather conditions were extremely windy. So we rowed a bit inside the harbor and then called it a day. That was it, our on-the-water training was done. We took the boat out of the water and felt more than a little defeated and disappointed. But it was a very good experience for both of us; it was good for Frank to build up confidence not only in himself but his confidence in me as well. I figured he would listen to what I had to say more in the future, men can be so stubborn!

After loading up the boat we said our goodbyes to Jo and set off for a road trip to Franck's hometown of Metz, France. Franck scheduled a series of interviews and presentations for us in Metz. The drive took forever because of the high wind conditions. Always against the wind!

When we arrived in Metz we were pleasantly surprised to see 200 colorful hot air balloons in the nearby park trying to lift off in hopes of breaking a world's record. (Metz, by the way, hosts the largest hot air balloon festival in Europe during the third week of September.) But the balloons were grounded and the event was canceled because of (go ahead and guess) the WIND! Two hundred hot air balloons rising up and floating into the blue sky would have been pretty cool to see. But we still needed to work the crowd, so we parked the boat outside the main hangar so people could see it coming and going. I noticed many people studied the boat, looking for any kind of information as to why a rowboat was sitting in a park surrounded by balloons, but we still hadn't even put her name, the website, or anything on it. One of the balloonists exclaimed "that will never fly" speaking about our rowing boat. This statement stuck in my head and later I would recall, as the boat was craned to the water, the flight of *Rowoflife*!

Some of Franck's family came there to help us and we put his kids to work handing out brochures. When they weren't playing on the boat, I gave them rides on my wheelchair. People must have thought it strange to see a person pushing a wheelchair with three kids all piled up on it. But what really got their attention was the 360° wheelies I did with all of them on my lap. More mad wheel chair skills!

For the rest of the day, we passed out brochures and talked to lots of people about ourselves, our Atlantic Row mission, and *Rowoflife*. Making appearances and giving speeches is not as much fun as rowing but they're still an important part of the job. By this time, I was feeling ready to get back to the gym and resume some kind of physical training. Too much rest and I always feel like rigor mortise sets in. But a few days of personal appearances, I felt, could only help our cause. Before I left, the organizers tried one last time to break the record for hot air balloons and Franck and I headed to the festival for our final presentation. There wasn't any rain that day but the strong winds forced every balloon to once again stay grounded. Not that many people attended the event and I began thinking what a waste of time our attendance had been.

Things happen or people come along and say just the right things at just the right time. We got so many rejections and so few positive comments that when it did happen, it was worth remembering. Just as we were getting ready to pack everything in, a small group of people with a young girl about eight or ten years old approached me. They were all curious, but the girl was so excited about the boat, so I told the mother that it was okay if she climbed aboard. While her daughter looked everything over inquisitively, the mother turned to me and said, "Thank you" and explained how she hoped that one day her little girl might decide to row across the ocean. It was the perfect ending to a trip that started off so rocky.

We finally finished our training and rounds of presentations and appearances on July 30, 2007 and I prepared for my return trip to California. If you think battling the wind and the waves are difficult, that's nothing compared to traveling when you're disabled; it always presents its own special set of problems and I never look forward to it. Frank took me to the train station on August 1 and I boarded the train for Paris, where I connected to another overnight train to Madrid, Spain. Unfortunately, the overnight trains with sleeper coaches were not wheelchair accessible and the corridors leading to the rooms were only about eighteen to twenty inches wide. Plus, I couldn't find anyone who spoke English and the rail personnel made no effort to find anyone who did; nor would they assist me in any way. It took me a couple of trips to handle my luggage and disassemble my wheelchair so I could get it through the corridor. My room was halfway down the length of the train the only way I knew how – I sat down, placed my things on my lap and I butt-scooted backwards down the corridor.

A young girl drew this picture of herself rowing the *Rowoflife*

My roommates in the sleeper coach made exiting the train in Madrid much easier by carrying my luggage and chair off the train for me. I taxied across the city to the other train station and boarded the train for Málaga, located on the northern side of the Mediterranean Sea. I phoned my friends when I arrived and they instructed me to take a train to the nearby town of Feugorila, where they would pick me up at the station. I had some difficulty with a security guard because he wouldn't let me board the train. No one in security spoke English very well but I'm pretty sure they said, "No disabled" (I guess the wide gate and elevator were for strollers and luggage carts.) I waited until that particular security guard wasn't looking to make it onto the subway and board the train. Once I arrived in Fuego-rila, I checked into the hotel, called my friends and we made arrangements for them to pick me up and drive me to the Malaga Airport so I could catch my flight to Heathrow Airport in London.

Flying when you're disabled presents its own set of problems, too. Depending on the airplane, I normally sit in the bulkhead so I can have enough legroom. However, when I checked in for my British Airways flight, I learned that I had a regular seat and wasn't allowed to change it. I boarded, sat in the assigned seat and, of course, I didn't have enough room for my legs, and I did my best to keep the seat in front of me from crushing them. I realized later that I didn't do such a good job because the meniscus in my left knee had been re-injured. I was so happy and relieved when that flight was finally over and I couldn't wait to get back into my comfortable wheelchair. But upon landing, I learned that the flight attendant was not allowed to bring my wheelchair to the gate.

Instead, they brought me a standard (or should I say substandard?) airport-issued wheelchair with very small un-wheelable wheels and an airport employee to push me. The chair was so old and rickety that I knew there was no way he could push that wheelchair around…and then I had to ask him to take me to the toilet. How humiliating and embarrassing. After those few awkward moments, I thought he would take me to the gate. Wrong. He took me to a room away from everything, had me transfer out of the wheelchair into a stationary chair and then he left with my ticket. I had been imprisoned.

British Airways had stolen my independence, my freedom, not to mention my dignity. Since I was trapped, I couldn't go to the toilet again or get food or shop or converse and relate to the other people who were traveling. I could do nothing but sit, wait and occasionally listen to and see the other people in the airport being FREE. As time passed, I wondered if they had forgotten about me. To pass the time, I entertained myself by taking out my video camera and making a series of small videos documenting my experience at the London Heathrow Airport.

After what seemed like a day and forever, I butt-scooted to the water dispenser, got a glass of water and heard voices in an adjoining room. I called out to them but there was no response. The voices silenced and I called out again; they were ignoring me, so I continued scooting to go check it out. When I entered, I held my water glass up in the air and announced that even prisoners get bread with their water! The airline personnel took one look at me and commented, "Well, if you wanted something, all you had to do was ask!" "I would like my wheelchair and to go to my gate!" I was not being belligerent, I was tearful. They continued to ignore me.

After everyone went back to what they were doing before I "barged" in, I made my way back to the "holding pen." Some more time passed and when airline employee's brought two more disabled people to the prison I had been forced to sit in all day, they looked shocked to see me. That's when I discovered that, yes, they had completely forgotten all about me. They put me in the little chair and took me to the gate arguing with each other the entire way there and even threatening to leave me at one point because it was not their job to take me. All I could think as I looked down on take off was ... Thank God that was over!

My seat, the crew, and the final flight home were good. Unfortunately, once I arrived at the Los Angeles Airport, I learned that British Airways had lost my wheelchair. Once again, I was plopped into an airport-issued wheelchair and carted through the airport, through customs, into the baggage claim, and out to the car. When I arrived home I had my partner, Debs, bring an old chair out from the garage and I used it until my chair was finally located and delivered three days later.

I didn't know that having a disability made us less human. It must be because people in general (and the airline industry itself) feel like they can make policies and rules that violate our human rights and take away the freedom and independence that our wheelchairs provide. This clearly is wrong and needs to be changed. People with disabilities are all uniquely different in their abilities. If a wheelchair user requests that their wheel-chair should be gate-checked for use for connecting flights and changing planes, then that request should be honored, not ignored. The freedom and independence that an individuals' wheelchair provides is essential for their safety and well being. In addition to the deprivation of food, water, toilet privileges, and human interaction the disabled person is at the mercy of others. What if there had been a fire or other emergency? What would have been our means of escape?

Events like that happen all too often; as much as I'd like to dwell and get angry, upset, disappointed or dismayed, I can't. Once a disabled person, or anybody for that matter, gets caught up in all the "you wouldn't believe what happened to me" self-pity, it can wear you down and hold you back. Sure, it's downright difficult to hold on for another day but think about the alternative – sitting around and doing nothing. That's no way for me to live. I refuse to hand over my power to somebody else. They can't hurt you unless you let them.

With the training in France behind me I could only look ahead and move forward … soon I would be heading off to Philadelphia for a week for National Rowing team training camp, then on to Munich for the World Championships.

CHAPTER 11:
QUALIFYING
IN MUNICH

When I arrived at the Olympic Regatta Course in Oberschleissheim near Munich on August 18, 2007 for the World Championships of Rowing, all I could think about was the 99 days Franck and I had left until we embarked on the Atlantic Crossing. Just one more monthly payment and our $32,000 entry fee would be paid in full. Our fundraising efforts weren't going very well and we were still coming up short sponsor-wise and dollar-wise. Franck mentioned that money may come in after the publicity of the race hits the media. But I couldn't really concern myself with it too much, because I needed to focus my attention on the next two weeks. Until the last race on September 2, my rowing partner and I had to concentrate on, if not winning, then certainly making a good showing in Munich.

I hadn't checked out the competition so I didn't know much about the other boats except that there were a total of 1,285 athletes racing as part of 474 crews; the biggest team hailed from the USA with a total of eighty-eight athletes and all of us were looking forward to qualifying for the 2008 Beijing Olympics and Paralympics. Since adaptive rowing would make its debut at the Paralympic Games in 2008, the World Championships in Munich included adaptive rowing for the first time as part of the qualification process. At last, my aspirations of becoming an elite athlete and dreams of one day competing in the Olympics were once again realized with adaptive rowing's inclusion in the Paralympics.

In order to make it to Beijing, only the top eleven boats in the men's single, pair, double, four, quad and the lightweight men's four and double would qualify. It's interesting to note that it's not the athletes who make it, it's their boat that qualifies. The rowers must then retain their spot on the national team and in that boat to be chosen for next year's Olympics. There are so many countries that only the fastest 11 can go.

All four existing adaptive boat classes were qualified and represented – the LTA (legs, trunk and arms) is a class for rowers with a disability who have the use of their legs who can use a sliding seat to propel the boat. The TA (trunk and arms) class includes rowers who have trunk movement but who are unable to use the sliding seat to propel the boat because of significantly weakened function of the lower limbs. And AS (arms and shoulders) class features rowers who only have the use of their arms and shoulders

One hundred fifty-two disabled athletes entered from twenty-three nations – an impressive 50% increase over the previous years, and my rowing partner and I knew that we had to work really hard if we wanted to make it to Beijing. I also knew that we had a giant bull's-eye on our backs and that everyone was gunning for us. In the six years that we had known each other, he and I had never lost a race – ever.

Our winning partnership began September 8, 2001 in Philadelphia at the Adaptive Rowing Nationals. He lost both his legs in a car accident in 1987, had been an active member in the adaptive rowing community for fifteen years. We met on the awards platform where he was awarded a gold medal and I had won the silver racing against him. It was a perfect opportunity to ask him if he would like to row thirty-seven nautical miles in the Pacific Ocean. At first, he looked at me like I was crazy and said no, but later he began asking questions about open water rowing. Mark Baiada, who sponsors Philadelphia's adaptive rowing event, overheard our conversation and offered him sponsorship for his participation. His answer quickly went from no to yes, and it was a done deal. Just a couple of weeks later, we teamed up for the Catalina Crossing, a thirty-seven nautical-mile race from Marina Del Ray, California to Casino Point, Avalon on the island of Catalina, about twenty-two miles southwest of Los Angeles. It was a perfect beginning to our adaptive double sculls association and a winning team was born...did I mention that we came in first place?

Six years later, and quite a few races and medals under our belts, we sat by the course in Oberschleissheim built for the 1972 Olympics waiting to begin the first of three races in which we were competing. As I looked out at the grandstands and marveled at the beautiful manmade course, I was pleased to see that there were more participants than ever before at this world championship event.

With so many disabled athletes competing, we knew that it was good for the sport but not so good for us; we discovered later that many of the competitors were minimally disabled rowers who had full use of their legs for bracing and pushing in a fixed seat. Because trunk and arms rowers are not supposed to have use of their legs, the powers-that-be felt that I had some sort of advantage and forced me to remove my braces so I couldn't put pressure on my feet. The truth was the other competitors in my class did not use wheelchairs and had great use of their legs and could walk and brace and push without orthotics. I had expected everyone in the Trunk & Arms class to have no use of their legs. It was, after all, a requirement for my classification. Did it mean that most countries, including the USA, needed to go out and recruit some minimally disabled athletes if we wanted to stay in the medal hunt? The beginning of every new sport seems to have the same difficulty with classification and we all wanted to bring more people to the sport but the powers-that-be drew the lines in the sand. Many of us who saw the injustice of it all were not permitted to protest and in fact, we were told not to make any waves at the beginning of the World Championships.

After noting the physical advantages of the other rowers, we knew we didn't stand a chance, but neither one of us said anything nor did I want to write anything about it. As much as I wanted to lead the protest parade, I just kept my opinions and thoughts to myself. I'm not planning to compete forever; and as a coach and an adaptive rowing program director, how I recruit or train my successor will be determined not by ethics but by the politics of sport. It is almost enough to make me want to quit. But I'm no quitter. We planned to return the following year after I completed the Atlantic crossing. The biggest pressure at the moment, of course, was getting the boat qualified for Beijing.

Two weeks and eleven heats later, we came in fifth, securing our spot for doubles in the Paralympics (allowing me to leave my braces on would have leveled the playing field and not left me at such a disadvantage). Although the USA Adaptive Team didn't score any medals in Munich that year we all qualified our boats for Beijing 2008; only four countries could boast that accomplishment.

CHAPTER 12:
ON OUR WAY TO LA GOMERA

After the championship in Munich at the end of August 2007, I flew to Paris and hopped on a train to Metz to meet up with Franck for more training with our boat, *Rowoflife*. After a couple of days meeting with media and potential sponsors, I got a chance to take a look at the boat. To my dismay, the boat still was in the same pathetic condition as it was when we trained in Lampaul in July. There was nothing new, nothing repaired, just a silent boat that spoke to no one. It had no sponsors, no information, and its name was nowhere to be seen. I was able to raise about $5,000 total over two years for the project which I spent on discounted rowing clothing from JL Design, custom oars from Concept2 and travel. Where were those logos? They were nowhere to be seen.

The boat remains silent and speaks to no one

How could we make any kind of statement or impression? From the looks of it, it was still just a blank, white, ocean rowing boat. Frank still hadn't even put the website or any other kind of information on it. Was he expecting me to do it? We were still trying to find sponsors. The thought of hustling to find money and sponsors with only a few weeks to go was discouraging but we still needed to train for the next two weeks.

After a short time of rowing in the Penfeld River, we soon realized that our rowing stroke was not very efficient. I needed to make some engineering changes to our rigging. I took my foot stretchers all the way out so that Franck and I could move to a more efficient location for rowing and moved us forward, closer to the pin. After I rigged brackets up to mount the foot stretcher to the life raft enclosure, we both had enough room to row efficiently; it made a big difference in boat speed. We had to rig the boat to make our rowing stroke as long as the others who could fully slide in order to compete with them. I wished I had made that change before our coastal row from Lampul to Brest.

There were a few people camping and fishing along the riverbank that had never seen or heard of an ocean rowing boat, so they were checking us out and waving as we rowed by. It was a Saturday so the park was busy with families, and the ever popular balloons were there. The river was also busy with rowers, kayakers, water skiers, jet skis and motorboats.

The following day, we took a class of children with disabilities, their teachers and aides out on the boat and let them take turns rowing. We were all having a great time and then I had to go and break the boat! I was at the helm and bringing us in a little too fast and at a bad angle; the corner of the dock wasn't padded and it pierced right through the plywood and punched a good-sized hole in the hull right above the waterline. *Rowoflife,* like most ocean rowing boats, is subdivided into watertight compartments and is fully self-righting and self-draining when the hatches are closed, so don't worry…we didn't sink!

———————

By now, it was November 19 and Franck and I only had nineteen days to the start of the 2007 Atlantic Rowing Race. It had been a long and difficult journey just getting to the starting line and we had invested and dedicated two years of our lives to this project. Our requests for sponsorship and support had been turned down and rejected by nearly everyone. This, and the lack of media response and interest, continued to be a shocking disappointment to us, but we never quit trying. We believed in ourselves and we had a gut feeling, an instinct that somehow we would get to where we needed to go!

We decided to dedicate our row to the pursuit of human rights and about the acceptance of people regardless of differences. Ironically, our differences seemed to have managed to get us rejected by everyone. All we aimed for was to inspire, motivate and affect positive changes in the lives of those who are born or made disabled and those who have suffered serious trauma in their lives. But somehow, we weren't getting any respect. I've said it before and I'll say it again, some of the reasons include the fact that I'm woman, an American lesbian woman, and a paraplegic at that, and because Franck's a straight Frenchman who's an amputee. Evidently, we had enough differences to offend everyone equally. Although no one stepped in to help or support us financially, we were even more thankful that no one tried to stop us and that we were allowed to participate in the event.

Somehow we had managed over the course of two years to buy the boat, and to pay our race entry fee. On November 20, 2007 with all of our documents in order, I left for La Gomera, the second smallest island in the Canary Islands, which lies just off the coast of North Africa situated between Morocco and the Western Sahara. Franck's plan was to drive the boat on a trailer through France and Spain and take the ferry over to La Gomera where we would meet up fourteen days prior to the race start date of December 2. There were still a lot of things working against us up to this point, but come hell or high water we'd be ready... all systems were go.

After I arrived in La Gomera, I checked into my hotel, placed my bags in my room and proceeded to the marina where the other entrants were busy preparing their boats. Each vessel was decked out with large, colorful graphics, sponsorship logos, and stickers of every size, shape and color. Like a kid who shows up on the first day of school in old clothes and worn out shoes, I felt the slight twinge of shame when I thought about our colorless, lifeless little boat. Not only was she a blank slate, but to top it all off, the last time I saw the boat, it was completely void of all of the equipment we needed for the crossing. We did not have a fixed-mount GPS, parachute anchor, drogue anchors, first aid kit, tool kit, new seats, new deck hatches, stainless hardware, shackles, swivel shackles, rope, a spare rigging kit or grab bags. Nor did we have spare parts kits for electrical components or for the watermaker. Franck was responsible for prepping the boat according to Woodvale's rules and regulations. Only, Franck didn't know how to prepare the boat – because all the information was written in English! I was hoping, even half expecting, that the boat would be ready when I saw it again. I thought that Franck was going to hire or would have enlisted help or had Jo help prepare the boat. That had been wishful thinking. It was beginning to get late and the last ferry had arrived and there was no sign of Franck.

The following day I wheeled around La Gomera mostly between the hotel, the boat yard and the ferry terminal looking and waiting for him. After not hearing a word, I began to worry thinking that something had happened to him or the boat. Even our competitors and Woodvale officials began inquiring about his whereabouts. There was a discussion among Woodvale officials that if he didn't arrive ten days prior to the race as required, then he and I would incur a penalty for every day he was late. I kept conjuring up all the "what ifs" like I usually do – what if he changed his mind, what if he was injured in an accident, what if Woodvale disqualified us or wouldn't let us race because of his tardiness? It was an extremely stressful time; could this be a repeat of what we went through in 2006? I don't think I could handle more disappointment?

No one had heard from him by the second evening and, instead of wallowing in the what ifs any longer, I decided to immerse myself in the festivities and go to Woodvale's Annual Fancy Dress Party. I know what you're thinking – rowers at a fancy-schmancy ball? But, in fact, it wasn't a red carpet, tuxedo only event; in the UK and other places in the world a fancy dress party is another name for a costume party. When I entered the room, it was a sea of pirates, naughty nurses, people in outfits scavenged from local thrift stores plus one imaginative rower who dressed up as an orca whale in black trash bags. I did not have a costume or any other nice outfit for the fancy dress party but it really didn't matter, I still fit right in and had a great time. I stayed up way too late talking to everyone about everything, answering questions, asking questions, and just getting to know everyone a bit better. I wished many times that Franck had been there that night.

The next morning Debs arrived. She had flown over from Long Beach to cheer us on and help us with the race. I was quite tired from the previous night's party but eager to get down to the dock to see if Franck had arrived. He hadn't, but I finally got word that his car suffered a broken trailer axle in Spain, which delayed his arrival at the ferry to the island by a couple of days. I guess it would be pointless for a guy who speaks only French to telephone someone who understands no French to explain why he was late…you could say language barrier, I say man thing!

By the end of the day, just as the sun was beginning to set, I saw him waving from the ferry. I was so excited to see his little European family station wagon drive off the ferry and laughed when I saw that it was loaded down so heavily with canned food and supplies that the weight of the trailer practically dragged on the ground. Then I became overjoyed when I saw *Rowoflife*. Not only was the United Nations flag proudly waving on the stern but the plain, white boat that spoke to no one just a few weeks earlier was now decorated with logos and on the bow was a graphic design of big, menacing shark teeth.

I wasn't familiar with Franck's sponsors, but I did know we used logos of organizations whose policies we support and believe in, not necessarily of sponsors who supported us financially. My sponsors were prominently displayed too – the logos included California Adaptive Rowing Program, Wheels2Water, Youth for Human Rights, my California Chapter of the

Paralyzed Veterans of America whose donation of $3,500 was the largest I received, Jo Ann Pine came in second at $1,000.00 and Robert Soto, a fellow veteran who donated $100. Sitting on the bulkhead was the logo for the Human Rights Campaign (the HRC didn't contribute anything to this project but I wholeheartedly believe in its mission to research, educate and encourage lesbian, gay, bisexual and transgenders to live their lives openly and to seek equality.) So there we were – two years, lots of credit card debt and many sponsor rejections later – standing in La Gomera together with our boat waiting to begin "The World's Toughest Rowing Race."

The broken axle on our trailer

The boat looked great, but it was far from what anyone would call ready. Franck apologized, explaining that he couldn't get the money or time off work to properly prepare the boat. Plus, the recent broken axle caused damage to the watermaker and most of the installations were prepared with screws and bolts that were not stainless (ocean rowing requires that everything be stainless and be installed with washers or support backing plates.) We had to replace all of the rusty screws and hardware with stainless. The stereo and magnetic speaker installation was right next to the compass so the large unshielded magnets interfered with the magnetic calibration of the compass. Unfortunately, it never worked the entire voyage. Not only were we missing a tool kit, a flare kit, the required parachute and drag anchors, rope, stainless hardware for use with the anchors, life line attached around the perimeter of the hull, and jack lines installed by the rowing stations, we didn't even have the required life jackets! On top of everything we had to do, I noticed that Franck hadn't replaced the rowing seats. After logging countless training hours, in addition to being used on two previous Atlantic voyages, the seats definitely needed to be replaced. Our rowing seats consisted of a piece of wood with two aluminum angle runners consisting of a right and a left rail, and were mounted between the two rails were small roller blade wheels that use bearings. The angle was way too thin, only about 1/16" thick and the mounting holes had worn and sheared off; the wheel could not be aligned properly and would rub against the side of the aluminum channel, which created resistance and drag, and the seats did not slide freely. This was not good and I had made it clear before leaving our training in France that the seats would need to be rebuilt before the row with at least 1/8" or 3/16" thick rails. For reasons I couldn't understand, he completely disregarded my advice, and even though I gave him specific details on how to rebuild them, he followed the suggestions of one of his friends instead. So there we were – stuck with those ugly, worn out, worn down, unusable seats. Unfortunately, the availability of spare parts for these seats was nonexistent in the region. We were stuck with them.

On the plus side, however, we did have a medical kit, two survival suits, two hand held GPS units, two personal EPIRB (emergency position-indicating radio beacons) tracking transmitters, a satellite phone, a boat position transponder, an underwater camera, a video camera with extra batteries, a portable solar charging mat and a few built-on solar panels.

Upon first inspection, it would seem as though we were screwed and didn't have the slightest chance of being seaworthy. The list of what we had to do and what we had to get was so long it seemed like mission impossible. The first item for repair was the bracket that mounted the watermaker. Franck began screwing the mounts through the boat below the waterline. I had one of those "oh shit" moments, but like the seats, it was pointless to say anything or be too angry. What was done was done and the solution to fix it meant mixing up some resin and catalyst and taking some carbon fiber cloth and patching over the countersunk screws hoping and praying that it wouldn't leak while we were out at sea. Don't get me wrong, I love Franck like my brother, he's a good man and I'm sure that I made plenty of mistakes, too, but, sorry to say, Franck didn't strike me as being particularly mechanical.

Every day Debs would take our shopping list, jump on the ferry and visit the various marine shops or stores and purchase everything we needed to repair, replace or stock the boat. Language differences compounded the degree of difficulty; although English was spoken on the island, the British had different names for boat parts. Unfortunately, it didn't really matter I guess because the shop clerks spoke only in Spanish. Debs spoke some Spanish but the translation or British name of the parts had no translation and Debs, not being a boater, didn't know the English word for the part anyway!

Franck and I continued to work feverishly day and night getting the boat ready for the safety officer who would come around and scrutinize our progress. In the middle of all this, I was getting sick with the cold or flu but we continued to work.

The food is usually the last thing inspected and loaded in the boat, so once we got most of the major repairs completed, we turned our attention to stocking up the hatches. Forget about serving up three hot, square meals; while at sea, a person eats for fuel. In addition to freeze-dried food supplies, Franck brought a lot of canned food but, unfortunately, we could only take about 40% of it because of the volume of liquid packed in each can weighed down the boat.

We loaded 90 days worth of food packaged according to calorie consumption of 5,000 calories minimum per day for each of us. We placed everything in sealed plastic waterproof bags, then wrapped all of it in plastic wrap and taped it all securely with massive amounts of cellophane tape. The packages were then carefully loaded into the deck hatches organized into a map or plan so that we could easily find every item.

Everything that needed to be gauged, wrapped, repaired, replaced, stored, stuffed, weighed or measured had been completed and we went off to bed that last night before the race feeling excited and eager. Franck's friends came in from France to help and see us off but didn't have a place to stay so Debs and I gave up our hotel room and went to the boatyard and tried to sleep on the boat. Normally, the sound of water can easily lull me to sleep but there were so many stray cats and mosquitoes that the constant hours of meowing and buzzing were a nuisance; so needless to say there was no sleep for either of us. I was still sick with the flu and exhausted, but on the other hand I was so excited that we had made it this far. There was no quitting and no turning back or giving in to any kind of illness. And as Franck would say it was time to "go, go, GO!"

CHAPTER 13:
THE ATLANTIC
RACE BEGINS

The morning of December 2, 2007 was cool and crisp, and the sky was clear blue. All twenty-two boats, consisting of two solos, fourteen other pairs and five fours teams sat in the water ready to go. With only two hours until start time Franck and I still had some last minute details to attend to. Some of the other participants came up to help and to assist in taking the boat off the trailer and putting it in the water. However, it was low tide and the ramp was so steep and slippery that we were unable to launch from the trailer and had to use the crane.

The Flight of *Rowoflife*

After we put it in the water, I rowed to the slip where Franck was waiting. We inspected the watermaker and discovered that it was non-operational. Everyone worked hard to get it going but we were running out of time. No watermaker, no crossing! There'd be no way we could make the voyage without making freshwater out of seawater and bringing water on board was not an option since a gallon of water weighs about eight pounds. After quite a bit of fiddling, race organizer and safety officer was able to bypass a non-critical step in the water making process and successfully produced safe drinking water for us.

It was just one hour until start time and we breathed a big sigh of relief. After everything was checked, rechecked and triple-checked, we were done. Everything was in place. Silently bobbing on the water, we just sat there; slowly and silently rising and falling atop the waves. Exhausted from all the preparation of the previous few days and feeling beat up from the last two years of struggling against the odds, we sat quiet waiting for the race to begin.

We could have used some extra rest and started later, but our stubbornness would not permit us that option. Besides, we had a lot to prove. Even with all the publicity, interviews, and press releases, nobody expected us to make it to La Gomera. Especially with all of the sponsorship rejections, everyone expected us to fail at every stage of the project. I have to admit, we had thoughts that we would come in last due to our physical limitations, but just finishing was our only expectation of each other and of our boat. Coming in first or last wasn't the point. My disability makes me strong and fills me with courage. It was amazing to think that if I succeeded, then I would be the first disabled female to row across the Atlantic.

We said our goodbyes to family and friends and rowed out to the start of the race with the other boats. We all bobbled around on the water anxiously waiting for the horn that would signal the rowers to begin while race organizers performed various VHF radio checks with each of the boats. When we were contacted, my throat was so hoarse from my recent bout with the flu and I couldn't speak; Franck only spoke French so when they called he didn't speak either. But we knew our radio worked, so we just ignored them.

The horn sounded at 12 GMT (4:00 am West Coast time) and the race was on. We began to row out of La Gomera!

The race start in La Gomera

A large number of yachts, fishing boats, and a fleet of oppys (little dinghies, specifically designed for kids up to the age of fifteen) from a local sailing school waved and cheered us on our way. It was an exhilarating send off!

I was still so sick. We worked so hard prepping the boat that our bodies were just beaten down. We rowed out and kept up with everyone until sunset but lost a little time when we decided to stop and eat. We lost sight of the other boats in the darkness and would not see them again the entire voyage. Since neither one of us could fully understand each other's language, things like performing tasks, having a meal or looking out at the ocean were mostly done in solitary silence. Franck had decided he would do the cooking and I insisted he maintain the seats. I took charge of the navigation and communication.

After we ate dinner that first night, we began our watch system of rowing two hours on and two hours off. As soon as I began the first rest shift, Franck woke me, saying that he was confused about our direction. The winds had changed, or should I say the direction of the way the flag was blowing had changed. Somehow Franck had turned the boat around and had rowed us in the wrong direction, into the wind and we were heading north rather than south. (In rowing it is always backwards and it was an easy mistake to make.) Our bulkhead boat compass wasn't working due to magnetic interference from the magnets in the speakers, so we used a smaller compass on deck. Reading a compass while rowing means you have to add 180 degrees so north is south and west is east and in this case, the winds, tides and currents were not favoring us.

We turned the boat back on a southwest course and continued rowing in our shifts. While Franck and I were just getting settled into our regular routine, the boat Titanic Challenge issued a mayday call on December 3 – crewman had been washed overboard by a giant wave. Although he wore a life jacket, he wasn't tethered to the boat. He spent 40 minutes in the water before one of the support yachts, following the fleet just in case of such an emergency, came to his rescue. In the coming days, *Titanic Challenge* and *Move Ahead II* would retire from the race. Franck and I checked and double-checked our supplies and emergency procedures. No way in hell were we going to be forced to give up or quit. The fatigue began setting in we were making such slow progress. Franck may have been suffering mild sea sickness from the beginning, but began getting sick enough to complain about it during the day and by nightfall he could no longer row. Franck had never gotten seasick before; the race organizers had warned us that many rowers who never get seasick often do in these events because of the stress involved.

It was second night of the "World's Toughest Rowing Race." With over 2,550 miles of Atlantic Ocean left to row, Franck was so sick, he was able to come out of the cabin, let alone row. I did not even attempt to wake him or make him row. I thought if I let him get some rest he could recover sooner. The winds increased and the sea became tumultuous with wave after wave crashing down upon me. I was surrounded by miles of ink black ocean in pitch black darkness, just barely visible about 60 miles behind us were the lights of La Gomera and a bit closer on the starboard or left side were the lights of a small island named El Hierro, which is about 118 miles southwest of La Gomera.

There was no amount of serenity that night, as it was mostly tempered with anxiety, as walls of water, invisible in the darkness, were crashing down upon me. Being that low to the water with the waves exploding over the boat, there is always a risk of being knocked overboard or even the whole boat capsizing or being violently turned over. I wore my life jacket with the built in harness and was attached to the safety cable that runs the length of the boat. Nearing exhaustion after having rowed all day and half way through the night, I knew I was going to have to stop rowing and rest. With no one being on the oar the risk of capsizing in the unpredictable waves increases. I did not know if I could go inside the cabin with Franck. Being fearful it would be too much weight in the stern I decided to deploy a drag anchor and stay outside.

The conditions were so bad and I was so cold I decided to put on my one piece survival suit. Sitting on my rowing seat I struggled as the boat was violently being tossed around. I had managed to get both legs in and then it became necessary to remove my life line leaving myself unsecured and in that instant I was struck by a big wave and was knocked up to and over the bow of the boat.

The strap on my survival suit got hooked on the spare oar stanchion long enough for me to get a hand on the boat. I quickly secured my line to the cable and curled up at the bow of the boat with the suit only half way on. This was my worst night of the trip but certainly not the worst night of my life. My life did not slowly flash before my eyes. Thinking about all that had transpired in my life leading up to this challenge was all I could do while huddled up on the bow of the boat, not knowing if I would see another sunrise.

I welcomed the daybreak, breathed a sigh of relief, gave thanks then I retrieved the drag anchor and woke Franck up to row. After his two hour shift he woke me up to row. I was exhausted after my miserable night on deck and there was no possible way I could row another shift without sleep. I tried to explain this to him. Not knowing whether he understood or not, just knowing he was not going to continue rowing, I deployed the parachute anchor so we would not go to far off course while I slept. We woke up and found ourselves near the island of El Hierro. As I began retrieving the parachute anchor, I discovered that the trip line, used to pull up the anchor, had somehow gotten tangled with the anchor line so the chute was not collapsing as it should.

The currents and winds were taking us right towards the shore so after contacting Woodvale and the race support vessel to let them know our situation, Franck and I worked together to pull the boat up to the anchor and collapsed it manually, got it untangled and stowed away. The support boat arrived just as we had finished. They followed us a short time to make sure we were ok. While they were following us, I had a serious discussion with Franck. It was the first time I had ever bothered expressing anger with him. He certainly wasn't rowing and I knew I could not keep rowing by myself. It was not a solo boat. We were in range to be towed in and we had the support boat right there "Either row or go home!" I argued. I grabbed the satellite phone and made him call his wife.

When our plan to row the North Atlantic with Jo Le Guen in 2006 failed, Franck "died an emotional death," as his wife refers to it. Failing this time could have more than likely devastated him. I don't know what his wife said to him, but it changed everything. I think she said, "Row or die!" It got much better after that point. Franck was still a bit seasick, but we were going in the right direction. Finally we were rowing!

Now before you think that Franck's being a baby getting seasick let me tell you, Franck is one tough bird. After being injured in a motorcycle accident at the age of 16, he endured seven years and thirty-one surgeries before having his leg amputated below the knee.

Franck never wallowed in self-pity or doubt. He's gone on to run marathons, climb mountains, and get married and start a family. I truly believed he would not quit on me. The support boat slowly sailed away and the sun began to set as we began our third night at sea. The sleep I got while on the parachute anchor was enough; I was finally getting over my flu and feeling better. We had adjusted to the vigorous work schedule and Franck was getting over his sea sickness.

Franck, phone home

After dinner, he handed me the survival suit as if I was going to sleep on deck again; he then turned and adjourned to the cabin for another good eight hours of blissful sleep. Oh hell no! I got very upset. He was being selfish, I told him there was no way we were going to make a crossing that way. I could not row the shifts all day and night while he slept. I only allowed it the one night because he was sick. When I was sick, I still managed my share of the rowing, boat maintenance plus taking care of all of his needs by allowing him the comfort and safety of the cabin to recover. I was totally pissed at this point.

Another night outside on the deck was out of the question. I told him if he didn't want to row that was fine, but, I told him, *he* could stay outside on the deck. He didn't budge. I think he pretended not to understand my English but I am sure it was more of a stubborn standoff. Not only did he refuse to row, he also refused to get out of the cabin. In one quick move, I slid right passed him, darted into the cabin and plopped right in bed. He still wouldn't leave. That was not the first and certainly not the last time that Franck refused to budge. (It reminded me of his stubbornness the night we rowed into the Port of Brest in that storm.) So we slept back to back that night, two people squeezed into a one-man bed felt like sardines in a can, but it was warm and dry.

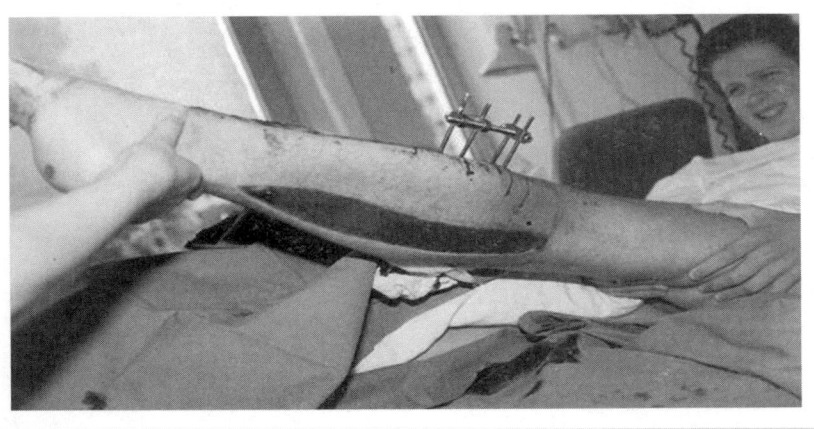

Franck in pre-op just before his surgery

With both of us in the cabin at the same time, I had reservations about the stability of the boat and feared that the boat would not track well in the waves if no one was rowing, so I made sure to put the drag anchor out off the stern. It wasn't necessary and it did slow us down but I did not know that at the time. We did learn later that we could both be in the cabin together and that it was not only ok for the boat but we could immobilize ourselves by bracing against each other so we could get better rest and recovery.

With the drama of who sleeps where resolved, we could go back to cursing El Hierro. We just couldn't seem to get away from the Canary Island's smallest island. Franck referred to them as the "Shit Islands" and the wind was "shit wind." After day three, we began rowing throughout the night and finally lost sight of the islands. We continued the two-on, two-off watch system while making our way south.

Franck in his survival suit

CHAPTER 14:
OUT ON THE
OCEAN BLUE

The new moon on the 9th and 10th of December made our evenings so dark that you couldn't see your hand in front of your face. So dark, in fact, that even the smallest amount of light would seem to pierce through the retina and cause physical discomfort. When we had nights like that, and there were many, we would turn all the lights off and run dark. Normally we had only a white all-round light and there was a light on the bulkhead compass we would cover. One night we happened upon a few whales that were curious about our little boat. They swam extremely close, so close that Franck and I thought that they would damage our little boat. It was too dark to see or to photograph them but we could hear them splashing, whistling and talking to each other so I took out the video camera and captured their high-pitched whistling and clicking sounds.

Occasionally, we'd both take a brief, but much-needed nap at the same time. Equipped with a radar detector that would sound an alarm if there was a boat near us, we felt safe grabbing our nap. But I don't know whether it was switched off, only understood French radar or, like most of our equipment, just was not working properly, but one day the alarm failed to warn us that a 1,300 foot-long behemoth of a boat was barreling down on us. Luckily, the noise and vibration woke us up. I looked up to see a Norwegian cargo ship beside us and its crew members were taking pictures of us.

The ship was well informed about the race so I knew they deliberately came over to see us and we were in no danger of a collision. In fact, they sent the pictures to the organizing committee. Franck and I had a meal while the container ship steamed away and then we resumed rowing. When word got out about our encounter, people were saying that it was a near collision…danger at sea; ocean rowers nearly crushed by Frigate… Drama! Yes, I was close enough to look practically straight up and see it, but that doesn't mean we were in any danger.

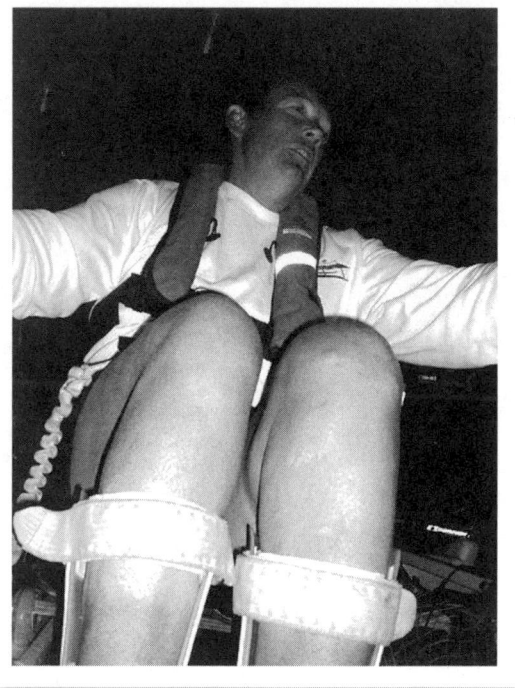

Rowing at night

Being surrounded by thousands of miles of ocean in the middle of the night can be very humbling and cathartic, but watching the sun set over the ocean is a marvel in of itself. With a sky as wide and as long as the ocean, you couldn't help but notice the shades of pink, yellow and blue slowly but intensely transform into orange, purple, crimson and gold. There were many days that the sun looked liked a huge red ball just hovering out there. In December, the sun moves farther toward the horizon each day and on the winter's solstice on December 22, it looked like it was standing still. Yep, I'd be looking at a lot of sunrises and sunsets over the next two months. The Geminid meteor showers, which peak on December 13 and 14 apparently offer some of the best light shows around with up to eighty meteors an hour. But I don't think I ever noticed; there were many times we saw things in the sky that we could not identify. We called it space junk but it could have easily been meteors.

On December 23, the planet Mars shined brilliantly right after sunset and I felt like our boat needed to shine a little, too, so I decided to decorate her with a couple of strings of solar Christmas lights. That night, a brilliant full moon shined down on us. All full moons at sea are spectacular and the light they provide give definition to the waves that crash down on you while you're rowing. In stark contrast to the welcoming light of a full moon is the ink-black darkness of a new moon. The waves come at you sight unseen, you can only anticipate that they will come, not knowing when or how, you just know that you will be knocked off your rowing seat. A couple of days later, Franck and I celebrated Christmas with dehydrated food and beer. After I gave Franck the presents that his family had asked me to give him, we called our families. Being away from family and the familiar sights and sounds of the holidays was tough, but at least we knew that we were being supported and loved.

A few days later, while I was at the helm, I noticed something trailing below the water line behind our boat. I thought to myself, did I forget to retrieve the drag anchor or did something blow overboard? I checked all of the lines and the anchors were in. Was it a shadow of a cloud? I looked overhead and the skies were pretty clear. No matter how far ahead I rowed, whatever it was kept straggling behind us. Was something floating in the sea? I stopped rowing and pointed out to Franck the big, ominous shadow hovering under the water's surface. Suddenly, a dorsal fin popped up. Shark! I quickly dashed to get my camera but when I was ready to take the picture it was gone.

Over the course of the next sixty days we'd see plenty of marine wildlife – dolphins, whales, sea turtles and many more sharks. One day, a sea turtle came up to our boat, raised its head up out of the water and nodded at Franck. It appeared to become so annoyed when Franck said something to it in French, that it pecked a couple of times at the boat and then swam away.

We listened to more than just the sounds of water and marine life. We shared music every day, and when we needed a little motivation and morale boosters, we really cranked up the tunes on my iPod or the boat radio, although we used it sparingly because it used too much power. One day the waves were perfect so I docked the iPod into the stereo and blasted the ocean with a great tune by The Sandals from the '60s film classic *The Endless Summer* while we surfed the boat over twenty-five foot waves. It was epic.

And there was always a moment to get creative – I even wrote a little song to the tune of the old TV show "The Beverly Hillbillies" that I played in my head more than once over the weeks…

> *A para and an amputee, they took a little trip*
> *Across the Atlantic Ocean and it wasn't a big ship!*
> *They scavenged through deck hatches, ate dehydrated food*
> *and they rowed every day when they weren't in the mood.*
> *Now that's ocean rowing…*

I taught Franck how to surf the boat and he seemed to really enjoy it. When we successfully caught a wave or two he would laugh like a giddy schoolboy. It motivated us, distracted us and relieved some of the boredom and stress. You can imagine how rowing everyday can be downright monotonous – "Ah, what will I do today?" you ask yourself repeatedly. "Oh, I know – I think I will row. And what will I do after that?" Hmm, I think I will row some more." It's not called "Row, row, row your boat" for nothing; I mean, that's all a person can do. We row day in, day out. Don't get me wrong; I was happy to be getting closer to the finish line, yet there was a longing for something different to do or to see.

The wind and seas really kicked up on December 29th, and it felt like we were riding a bucking bronco. I fell off my seat (damn those seats!) and bruised my back when I fell on Franck's foot stretchers. I couldn't do anything but crawl around on the deck; I couldn't even row. This happened just before we had three days of gale force winds blowing us in a good direction. Timing was such that I was able to immobilize myself by wedging between the side of the boat and the seat rail.

Resting on deck

When the conditions became good for rowing again, my back was good enough to resume. For a couple of days there, Franck would help me put my braces on and help me get to my rowing seat. Storms and rough seas were commonplace. Wind speed and directions would be forecasted for eight, twelve, twenty-four, thirty-six or forty-eight hours, but were really unpredictable.

After one such storm, Franck encountered a bird on our boat. It had landed on deck seeking shelter. Franck thought it was injured and wouldn't survive, but I took my tech towel, wrapped the bird to warm it up and placed it in a bucket. After about ten minutes our feathered guest began moving around and getting antsy. I un-wrapped the little bird and held it up on one finger and released it. At first it couldn't fly very well and Franck wasn't sure if it was going to make it. The bird fell or touched down into the water a couple of times but eventually it made flight; when we finally realized that it was going to make it safe and sound, I could see the joy in Franck's face.

A baby swordfish once jumped on the deck and we made a pail of water for it and took pictures of our passenger before releasing it.

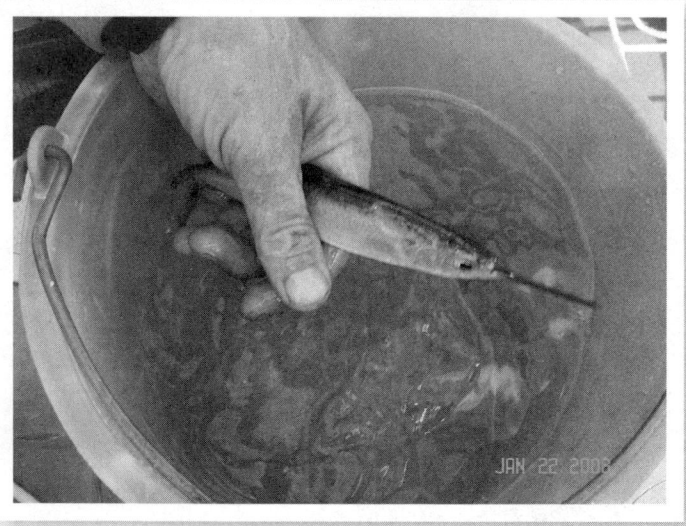

A billfish that had jumped on deck

We had only delayed the inevitable; almost as soon as Franck put it back in the wild a big fish caught it and swallowed it up. From then on every time we saw big fish jumping in and out of the water, we wondered what was out there chasing them. I read somewhere that there are about 210,000 marine life forms swimming around in 326 million trillion gallons of water! Arthur Clark was right, "How inappropriate to call this planet Earth when it is quite clearly Ocean."

We had many encounters with flying fish, too. We were so low to the water that collisions with these bony fish were inevitable. Ranging from one to ten inches in length, they can launch like rockets at speeds of up to forty miles an hour! It can be pretty scary when they strike you at night in the dark and they can give you a pretty good wallop when you least expect it.

These little flying fish pelted us repeatedly

One day we had emerged from the cabin to find our boat covered in the remains of dozens of flying fish. They were everywhere and we spent a good part of the morning throwing them overboard and cleaning up the deck. A day or so later I noticed an odor emitting from Franck's prosthesis.

Amputee sockets and prosthetic parts can get pretty stinky, so when I pulled it out to try and locate the source of the odor, I discovered a flying fish in his socket. Franck asked what the English word was for "the fish responsible for the foul-smelling odor." I chuckled to myself when I told him that it was "air freshener." I thought it was funny but Franck didn't get it.

Believe it or not, neither one of us found it absolutely necessary to speak each other's language in order to do the job we needed to do. Franck and I became as close as siblings. I am his sister of rowing and he is my brother of rowing. No one gets along 100% of the time, so neither of us had that expectation. I'm sure he was unhappy with me as many times as I was with him. He would even try and teach me French and he wanted to learn English.

There were times when we were in some pretty rough seas and there wasn't a time when the water was flat; actually, three to four foot waves were as flat as it got. On New Year's Day, the wind was blowing a different direction than the swell. How did it know that I celebrate January 1st surfing with all my friends back in Long Beach? The water was choppy and not very good for rowing but the wind churned up some gnarly waves, perfect for boat surfing. We guided the boat on the waves with the oars and caught a dozen or so good rides. I tried to teach Franck a few surfing terms and "dude" seemed to sound particularly funny with a French accent. Our language differences sometimes made me laugh and sometimes made me nuts.

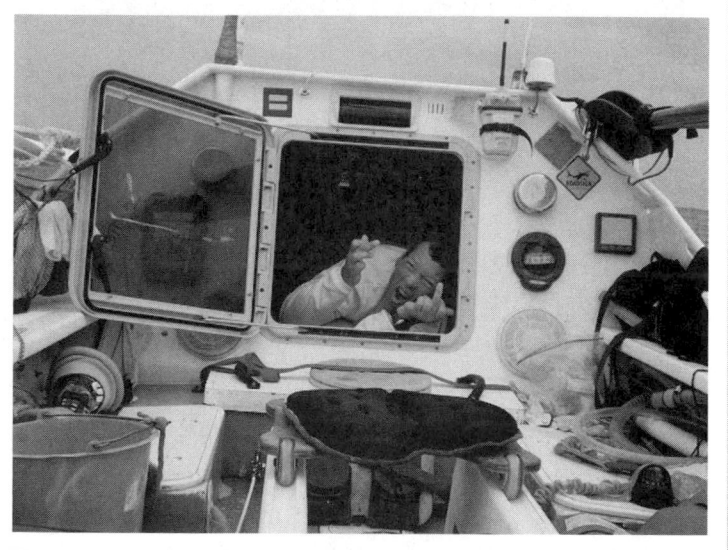

The middle finger in English

Sometimes, I used this language barrier to have a little fun. One day, a cluster of rain clouds came over the boat and Franck pointed up and called out in French, "nuage." When he asked me for the English translation, I jokingly replied, "piss on you" so you can imagine my delight when one day it began raining and he pointed up and yelled, "Piss on you!"

When Franck didn't really understand something he would simply shrug and say, "Normally, it is ok, Angela." And it never really bothered me, but once when the stanchion, which is an upright bar that provides support for the oars, had shifted, the spare oars had dropped down and there was no room for either one of us to row. He just shrugged, "Normally, it is ok, Angela."

The equivalent in French

More than once I tried to explain to him that they needed to be repaired before he could row but he always repeated those same five words. I tried two more times, but finally decided to let it drop when he became so frustrated with the lack of communication that he pulled extremely hard on the oars and smashed his hand into the spare oars that had fallen down. I probably should have been nicer but my response was a chuckle and to say, "Normally it is OK, Franck!"

Although we never had any major issues involving communication or the language differences, there was, however, the issue of the rowing seats. Since he hadn't listened to me and had completely disregarded my advice the broken down seats came back to bite him in the ass. If the seats don't move freely and there is resistance of any kind over a 3,000-mile row, you can suffer serious injury to your legs and hips. The seats became a big regret for both of us. I think I was angrier with myself for not just taking the seats home with me from our training and repairing them myself. I just trusted that he would take care of the seats. When the seats needed minor repair work, I would give him the tools and parts and tell him it was his to fix. He never really admitted he had made a mistake, but he knew why the seats were his responsibility.

Eventually, he did learn to trust me and learned to listen better. It is very important to trust and have some amount of faith in your rowing partner's abilities or knowledge. On January 2, day thirty-one of the Atlantic Rowing Race, Franck and I hit the 1,000-mile mark. Only 1,552 more to go!

CHAPTER 15:
ROWING INTO THE
HISTORY BOOKS

E ven with all the many fantastic sunrises and sunsets, encounters with marine life and riding the waves, the experience was as painful as it was beautiful. After a month in the open sea, everything was covered in salt, and we were covered in sores and rashes. Much of the time it was more comfortable to row naked as clothing was so saturated with salt it was abrasive to the skin.

The best relief from salt saturated clothing is to row naked

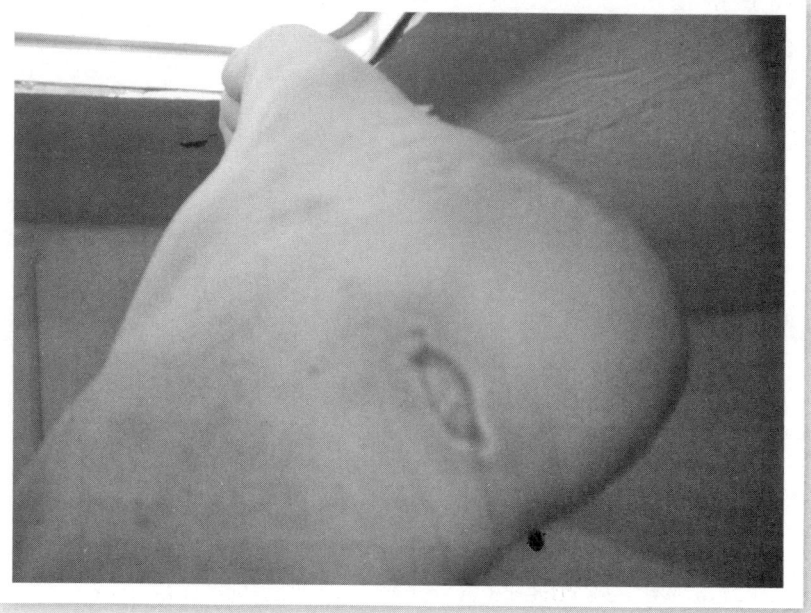

Sore caused by my orthotics

The braces made sores on my feet and my ankles. Healing is a slow process and infections are a major concern on the ocean.

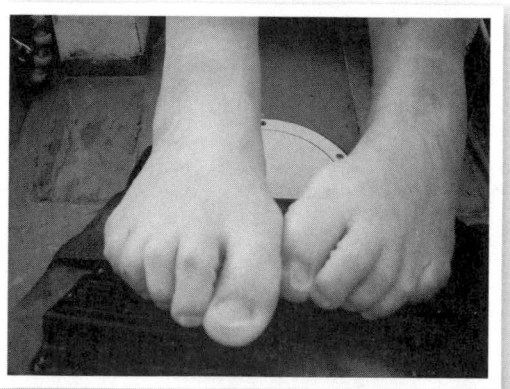

Salt water and friction caused these sores on my toes

The sores on my toes became so badly infected that Franck thought we would have to amputate them. On my lower half and feet, my greatest concern was infection. I took oral antibiotics specifically for that purpose and I cut the toes out of my shoes and made holes in the soles so seawater could drain out and air could circulate to my wounds. Eventually, my feet healed but sores would heal and new ones would appear. I was continuously cutting blisters and calluses off of my hands. On my hands they became so thick that they were irritating the tendon sheaths causing inflammation and tendonitis.

Blisters and fungal infections on my hands

More than once, my fingers locked up and I experienced so much arthritic pain in my hands that it became difficult for me to perform even the smallest of everyday tasks. In this damp, humid climate, fungal skin infections were common and most uncomfortable. Franck had a horrible fungal skin infection in a very bad place. I felt so bad for him. Oh, sure, we had a full medical kit on board but never used it because all the pharmaceuticals were filled in England and, just like the names of boat parts, the names of them were different and unfamiliar to me so I was afraid of trying anything. Even though it's always essential to have a medical kit on board, this one was pretty useless to us. I would make containers of desalinated water so he could soak his parts and get some relief. We were coating ourselves with Vaseline or petroleum jelly to try and make a barrier against the salt water.

Working, living, eating, and rowing together was a 24/7 equal opportunity proposition and we found it easier to even sleep back to back next to each other, although bunking side by side was anything but a dream. I named the inside of the cabin the mosh pit.

We named the cramped cabin the "mosh pit"

Two people sleeping and occupying the cabin space that's designed for only one person should expect to get slammed around a little bit. But we discovered that when we slept back to back, which kept us practically immobilized, we had a much better rest and recovery. We devised a unique rowing schedule that seemed to work for us – we would stay to the oar when the winds threatened to blow us off course, but if the wind blew us toward the finish line, then we would both sleep and check every two hours to see if the conditions had changed. Sometimes we would row twelve to eighteen hours and only sleep for four. But, of course, the more rest we got, the further we could row.

When we weren't rowing, eating or sleeping, we'd take pigeon baths, which are similar to a birdbath – we'd stand over a saucer of fresh water and splash ourselves like a bird in a puddle until we felt, at least, somewhat clean.

I phoned Debs every day with the *Rowoflife* blog entry and she would give us an update on the other boats in the race. Our blog described what we did or saw that day, what we broke or experienced what we repaired or retired. We would talk about what we missed and what we wanted most when we made land.

As each day passed, we got further and further ahead and found ourselves up to seventh place. The boats trailing behind us made their mission to barrel down and pass us. "The next boat to catch is…*Rowoflife*," the crew from the Atlantic Jack blogged. "This will be a tough one although they only have one fully functional leg between the two of them…they are complete rowing animals." It was great when I learned that other boats would also blog about trying to catch us, which motivated us to row faster and to stay the course.

We remained in seventh place for a very long time, even though we still didn't have a working compass and down to only one functioning handheld GPS, so we watched the latitude and longitude numbers to determine our direction of travel. It was too difficult to continually stare at the handheld, so we took our hand compass out of the grab bag and mounted it with epoxy to a place where we could both see it to establish our direction of travel and then note it on the compass. We rowed off that compass until the winds or conditions changed and we ran the numbers every couple of hours just to check. Other crews asked us how we could keep such a straight course. All of this was very flattering but none of it went to our heads. We were just doing the best we could, which is what we wanted to do all along. Doing our best meant being happy with what we were able to achieve.

The food we brought with us consisted mostly of dehydrated meals so we had plenty of bottles of Tabasco sauce to improve the flavor. We also had snacks of chocolate, licorice, candies, beef and salmon jerky. Franck brought a few special treats like a tin of Pringles potato chips and some cookies but hid them in the cabin deck hatch where I wouldn't see them, not because I would eat them but because they weren't packaged well and were not the best things to bring. His plan backfired when the cabin flooded and ruined his stash. The race people told everyone to keep the hatches closed no matter how hot and uncomfortable it got in the cabin. Lesson learned the hard way, I guess. Even though it was winter it was so hot on the ocean that some of the sweets and hard candies that Franck brought disintegrated and made a big sticky mess.

So much of ocean rowing is out of a normal person's comfort zone. There is so much discomfort in the physical demands and so much testing of the psychological and mental challenges. Some days just never seemed to end and time would overrun itself. When you're crossing an ocean, it's very easy to lose your sense of time and not even know what day it is, so we kept track by counting the days at sea by making a mark with a pen on the side of the boat.

Just two days from the finish line, we got stalled in a current and taken off course a bit. At the same time, the iPod was inoperative and we had run out of Tabasco. It was depressing thinking we had come so close and it felt as if we were not going to make it. I know that a media player and a condiment may not be a big deal on land where you're inundated with distractions, but after almost three months on the open sea, music and hot sauce count as mandatory necessities!

Franck did not even want to try to row us out of the current so I convinced him to steer an angular course with the rudder while I rowed with one oar. We managed to escape the current and move on, but not without adding another couple of days to the journey.

We both experienced prolonged bouts of sleep deprivation, which lead to extreme pain and physical discomfort. The ocean was always moving and so were we. It was by far the most physically difficult thing that I had ever done. Mentally, it still did not measure to having my surgery botched and losing everything.

About seventy miles out, we could begin to see the island of Antigua. But night was falling and we wanted to arrive in the morning or as soon as there was a speck of daylight. At fifty miles, out we began contacting the race organizers. In the last day of the trip, we dropped to eighth place and at twenty miles out, we were to call the race duty officer so they could prepare an escort boat to guide us into the harbor. Overnight, we got closer and in the morning I contacted them when we were five miles from the finish. But the tides and current were pulling us away from the mouth of the harbor so we ended up about one mile off the coast. With the end so close in sight, Franck and I rowed harder and harder, faster and faster. A race official motored out to meet us at the GPS finish line's predetermined coordinates. We were greeted like heroes – horns blared as we crossed, cheers filled the Caribbean air and people were taking lots of photos. Franck and I stopped rowing, dropped our oars and grabbed each other in excitement as press, family and friends took photos. The Woodvale race officials offered us a tow in but we declined. We had not rowed across an ocean to be towed in at the finish. The winds had once again decided to blow hard against us and we worked for three hours just to get into a harbor that nearly everyone could do in half an hour. Damn shit wind!

Once inside, the harbor boats honked their horns, and even more people cheered. Woodvale personnel lit flares to guide us to the dock. And once we landed they popped a champagne cork spewing champagne on our heads while yelling a cheer.

The finish line in Antigua

Franck and I had to wait for our people to bring us our things before we could get off the boat. Franck's dad was there with his crutches and

Debs was there with my wheelchair. We exited *Rowoflife* exhausted but exhilarated. Franck's first words to Debs were, "My dick and my bubbles are shit!" I silently remembered the other English question on the boat. As Franck placed them in the water to soak he asked "what is this?" in English, so I responded that it was his dick and his balls. I did not say bubbles but I let it go because it was pretty funny.

Debs had a "what the hell?" look on her face, but later as she became familiar with his medical condition, she understood. After all of the hugs and tears, they brought us the fresh fruit and beverages that we had requested. I had an ice cold soda pop and Franck had a beer. We sat and were interviewed by local media with family and friends close by.

Reunited with my wheelchair at the finish of the race

A cold bottle of Coke felt good on my blistered hands

Franck enjoying a beer at the finish

Everyone congratulated us and we posed for a group picture with the other boats that had come in before us. Debs got us a hotel room that, unfortunately, didn't have hot water but some new friends invited me to take a bath in their house and I happily accepted.

Debs and I slipped into her rented car and followed them up the wrong side of the road, dodging goats and chickens on the winding mountainous road to the top where sat the most beautiful house with the most amazing view. When we arrived, they showed me to the bathroom where there was a big claw bathtub positioned to view 180 degrees of the island and the Atlantic Ocean. Debs drew me a hot bath. I slinked into the tub and fell asleep.

On February 7, 2008, at the age of forty-seven, I rowed into the history books by becoming the first disabled woman to ever row across the Atlantic Ocean by oar. Frank and I completed the 2,550 nautical mile journey in 66 days, 23 hours and 24 minutes. Who would have thought that two people of two different ages, speaking two different languages, from two different countries would finish in eighth place in the pairs boats and tenth place overall.

How the boat gets to and from a race

Purchasing a trailer in Miami for *Rowoflife*

The next day Franck and his father cleaned the trash out of the boat and got it ready to ship. Knowing that I would use the boat to teach disabled kids to row and to offer them greater opportunities, he decided to give me the boat and I shipped it back to the U.S. Orlando Rogers of "Go Commando" was instrumental in helping us get the boat shipped home. He was so funny as he gave Debs instructions, he said to go to the slipway and see "Fat Boy," blushing and apologetically explaining that it is okay to call him that because that is what everyone calls him. Orlando was wise beyond his years and had such great manners, Debs and I both thought, "Wow this guy is awesome, his mother raised him right!" With his help instructions we were able to get the boat in the container and placed on the ship to Miami.

Rowing west, towards and chasing the sunset everyday on this epic journey has had such a prolific effect on both of our lives. Every sunset now transports me back to the ocean rowing boat, remembering how a few minutes every day we would stop rowing and listen to the sounds of the sea and the wind and quietly watch the sun setting across the horizon.

CHAPTER 16:
LIFE AFTER THE 2007 ATLANTIC ROWING RACE

M ark Twain once said, "It's no wonder that truth is stranger than fiction. Fiction has to make sense." My life has been hard to believe at times and seems like a made-for-TV movie and sometimes it has been hard to bear. But as I was writing in my journal, that would eventually become this book, I continued to discover more and more about myself relative to the answer to the question most people ask: "Why would you want to row across the ocean?" It's not that I'm being illusive when I say this, but I guess the simple answer is that every week of training, of waiting, of writing, of working towards the starting line, and wondering about the finish line, I learned more about myself.

The deep, underlying, up close and personal reason or purpose for taking on such a challenge has yet to be fully realized. Sure, there is the list of reasons why someone would want to row the ocean blue and I suppose that a person can go towards a dream or goal motivated by the list only, never realizing anything more, but there is more. Those people would not have an answer beyond that list. I am in a continual state of self-discovery and hope to maximize the benefits of the experience by learning all that is possible from it, which is a reason in of itself. I have found that my faith and my abilities are far greater than my doubts and my fears.

I couldn't have done everything by myself, yet it had to start with me. No one was going to take me by the hand and help me get on with my life – I had to do it myself. One important lesson I learned through all my years of rehabilitation, of striving, and winning – if you don't paddle your own canoe, you don't move. You row or you die!

In the years after the 2007 Atlantic crossing, I would achieve and accomplish more than I could have ever imagined. The following year, I placed first at the 2008 U.S. Rowing National Championships and then went on to reach the highest level that one can reach in sport – my Olympic dream became reality. After qualifying in Munich, I traveled to Beijing to compete in the 2008 Paralympics. We didn't win a medal (we came in fourth missing the medal round by nine-tenths of a second, and finishing seventh overall), but that wasn't the point. Getting up and going positively forward was, and remains to be, the point of my existence.

Another record was set in 2009 when I became the first woman to row across the Indian Ocean. Not only did my *Indian Ocean 8* crew mates set the world record for the fastest time (fifty-eight days!), but we garnered a spot in the *Guinness Book of World Records*.[1]

After 58 days 15 hours and 8 minutes it became the fastest crossing of the Indian Ocean by oar and the first eight person mixed crew. Helen Taylor and I became the first women to row across the Indian Ocean and I became the first disabled woman to not only row across the Indian but to have rowed across two oceans.

To explain briefly what ocean rowing is like I have often said that it is like a combination of two sports, rowing and bull riding extended over time and distance. A rowing race may last four minutes, a bull ride only two minutes. Ocean rowing is like trying to do everything including

---

1 The first sixteen-man crew to row any ocean was that of the *Big Blue*, which crossed the Atlantic east to west from Tarfaya in Morocco to Barbados in the West Indies, in 47 days 18 hours, from 15 January to 4 March, 2011. The skipper, Angela Madsen, and boat builder David Davlianidze (Georgia) were joined on board the vessel by Ernst Fiby (Austria); Ryan Worth, Elizabeth Koenig, Aleksandra Klimas-Mikalauskas and Louise Graff (all USA); Liam Flynn (UK); Steve Roedde, Nigel Roedde, Dylan White, Zach Scher, Charles Wilkins and Sylvain Croteau (all Canada); Thomas Butscher (Switzerland/Canada); and Margaret Bowling (Australia)..

eating, sleeping and rowing while riding a bull twenty-four hours a day, from one point of land across thousands of miles of deep ocean water to another point of land, taking months to complete.

There are no support boats and all food and supplies are carried on board. Solar panels charge batteries which operate a desalinator, or water maker, to remove salt from the ocean water and filter it for human consumption. We eat dehydrated food. We have a satellite telephone, VHF radio, GPS navigation. There is no plumbing or toilet. There is only a bucket.

A pairs boat is about 24 ft long, 6 ft wide and weighs about 1600 lbs fully loaded. The eight is 36 ft long, 6 ft wide and 2100-2500 lbs loaded. The pair is a sculling boat and there is an oar for each hand, two oars for each rower; the eight is rigged for sweep rowing, or one oar per rower alternating port and starboard.

There are squalls and storms generating high winds and huge waves. There are sores from salt, blisters from rowing, arthritic pain, other injuries, pain from falling and being knocked off the rowing seat and fatigue. It is dangerous and there is a category of missing at sea just for ocean rowers. I know it doesn't sound like much fun but there is no feeling like successfully completing an ocean crossing. I don't know quite how to describe it. It is putting yourself on the seat every day and doing the job, ignoring how you feel and doing what matters. It tests and pushes you to the limits both mentally and physically.

After doing so well in the Atlantic race, Woodvale asked me to skipper the crew of eight across the Indian having the most ocean rowing experience. It did not matter to them that I am a paraplegic. Unlike my other row with Franck, I was the only physically challenged athlete on the crew. Opportunities don't just present themselves for no reason, so I could not pass it up!

We had challenges from the beginning with the boat not being ready, the food not being purchased and the last minute crew changes. It is a pay-for-place concept and we all met for the first time in Australia. We did not know each other or train together before the crossing.

On day three of our Indian Ocean record setting rowing attempt we suffered a knock down as a large wave struck our boat from behind. Our steering system seemed to turn us prematurely as we were accelerating down the face of a massive wave. We ended up turned sideways as the wave crashed over us. A knock down is not a capsize as the boat never goes all the way over; it is more like being just at the point of rolling and then coming back the other direction. We had broken and lost some oars and one of our proper rowing seats was also lost in the chaos. Everyone was tethered to the boat so, thankfully, we did not lose any of the crew.

The solution we found to the problem of the lost rowing seat was to take a wooden plank or cover from the battery compartment and make a fixed seat. Having trained and competed as a fixed-seat rower for the last ten years, I volunteered to dedicate myself to that rowing position for the remainder of the crossing. The alternate watch had decided to rotate, and every day a different person would have to row from the fixed seat. Every-one agrees that it was the worst seat in the boat, being a wooden plank and not a proper rowing seat for starters. People really did not train to row with their backs and arms so it was quite a painful experience for them, not that it wasn't quite painful for me as well. But I just knew it was not going to cause me any debilitating injury or prevent me from being able to continue. I could also generate more power from the fixed seat having all of the experience and training that I have. I suffered the worst sores of the whole crew on my buttocks as a result.

Our auto pilot/steering system eventually failed and our crew who had sailing experience built a tiller system for steering the boat. This meant our watch system had to change again. To try and keep four people at the oar and one steering the boat, we had to alter the fixed-seat rowing station and make a place for the helmsman. I did this by removing the foot stretcher and making a new one from another wooden hatch cover from inside the cabin. It wasn't a sturdy system and we would often be knocked off the seat; but it worked well enough. We could then have our regular watch of four-plus-one. When we began it was two watches of four and twelve hours of rowing with twelve hours of resting. As we got closer to the finish and the steering went out we went to three rowing and one steering, keeping to the four-and-four. But people were not utilizing the rest periods in the excitement after we crossed the half way point and the boat was not moving as quickly with only three rowing, so we went to the four-plus-one, rotating in and giving up some of our rest periods. The boat speed increased and we made it to the finish in Mauritius ahead of all of the other boats in the race. We had given the Woodvale race participants a nine day head start, so to be the fastest across they would have had to come in nine days ahead of us.

This having been my second ocean crossing, comparing the two and noting the differences, this was by far the most difficult. There really were no favorable conditions and it was a farther distance. Then there were the people and personalities to deal with. Resolving all problems of all types quickly seemed to be the winning ticket even if the resolution was to ignore something, stuff it down or let it go all together. When we set out I had told everyone that no one gets along 100% of the time, even the best of friends, I believed that this helped as no one had the expectation that we would all get along. I did not get along with everyone on the boat but I showed no favoritism one way or the other to anyone. I put our experienced ocean rowers in charge as the watch captains and it wasn't perfect. I don't believe I would ever choose to do it the same way again, although it was a fantastic experience!

Out in the Indian Ocean

Indian Ocean crew (left to right): Bernard Fissett, Paul Cambell, Ian Couch, Doug Tumenello, Hellen Taylor, Brian Flick, Simon Chalk; (front) Skipper Angela Madsen

In June of 2010, three able-bodied women and I became the first female crew to row around Great Britain. Margaret Bowling was putting a crew together for the Circumnavigation Race around Great Britain. She messaged me and asked if I would participate. Somehow it became someone else's project but I stayed on anyway.

Although shorter than an ocean row, British waters are colder, rougher and busier and we had tides to contend with all of the way. To avoid the effect of the tides meant either rowing further offshore and lengthening the route, or staying closer in and stopping on anchor when making no forward progress as well as potentially battling against strong overfalls, standing waves and other tidal effects. We chose to stay closer to shore.

We set off from Tower Bridge in London on a grey, cold, dismal and typically British summer day, racing against a team of four men in a trimaran rowing boat named *Orca*. The guys dropped out soon after the start, close to Lands End.

Life in coastal water is very tough and we had a number of near misses with ships, including one where I sustained a significant injury to my hand from the kick back of a flare gun. Tolerance and understanding are key to success but being stuck in such a small space often tested these strengths to the limits. There were times when I was reaching the end of what I could realistically bear and I did consider giving up, then decided to stick it out for a bit longer, and a bit longer still. After 51 days, 16 hours and 42 minutes at sea, often stuck on sea anchor due to changing tides and inclement weather conditions, we rowed triumphantly up the Thames and across the finish line at Tower Bridge to become the first women to row around Britain.

In June, 2010, three able-bodied women and I became
the first female crew to row around Great Britain

Sir Richard Branson and Angela Madsen
Photo by Debra Madsen

The event was sponsored in part by Virgin, and we even received a letter from the chairman of the company, Sir Richard Branson, congratulating us on our accomplishment:

> *Go Seagals!!! I knew I was right to back the girls in beating the boys in the first ever Virgin GB Row and I'm over the moon that such brave women have achieved a World Record in such a spectacular fashion!*
>
> *This is why we set up the Virgin Trophy—Belinda, Angela, Laura and Beverley have pushed through extreme tiredness, hunger and serious injury to battle on and achieve the goal they set out to achieve.*
>
> *Britain has something to be proud of this summer after all!*
>
> —*SIR RICHARD BRANSON, Chairman Virgin Group*

Since I began writing this book, I rowed the Atlantic a second time in 2011, this time from Morocco in northwest Africa to Barbados in the Caribbean.

I dream big and set goals for myself realizing possibilities and potential for success, being hopeful and willing to do what is necessary to achieve those goals. When I first learned of the sport of Ocean Rowing I was drawn to it. I knew I was going to row an ocean. I did not, however, know that I would become such an accomplished ocean rower/adventurer. I did not allow the situation of being a woman and a paraplegic stop me. I just had to work harder and work differently to achieve my goals.

I was on the first Ocean Rowing Catamaran with a crew of sixteen to row 3000 miles across the Atlantic Ocean in an attempt to break the Atlantic world rowing record. It was my second time to row across the Atlantic nonstop and unsupported.

My becoming involved with the Big Blue project and crew was the result of taking a visually impaired rower from Canada, Franck Polari, ocean rowing in one of my Introduction to Ocean Rowing classes I taught at the Long Beach Rowing Association. It is not advertised any place, people interested in trying the sport generally contact me via e-mail. I took him out on a coastal row from Long Beach to Dana Point.

The project that he was part of had lost their skipper so he told them about me. I began receiving e-mails from Steve Roedde asking me to skipper their boat. I looked at what horrible financial shape I was in from ocean rowing without sponsors, gave much thought to my solo ocean rowing project and decided what the Hell!

First thing was to jump right in and organize sea trials for the project in order to make sure it happened, as this crew had been let down and abandoned before. They were not prepared, much of the critical information they needed to ensure success of their project was missing. I signed on late in the game with some big challenges ahead. We started a Google group and a mass of e-mail correspondence began. I organized a sea trial and some sea survival training for the crew on Shelter Island, New York. I traveled there and met the crew and David Davlianidze, the boat's builder, for the first time. After sea trials I returned to Long Beach. David worked frantically to prepare the boat and make arrangements to ship it. I continued preparing the crew and myself for the crossing. As skipper, besides keeping everyone as safe as possible and making the decisions of navigation, watch system, schedule and maintaining a good working relationship with the crew, there is caring for the crew; making sure they have what they need to do the job—enough food, enough water, enough rest. Making sure they are all healthy and well. I also needed to ensure they cared for themselves and each other, and not just physically. What we do out there is so tough and people can get so worn down that they need to be lifted up with praise and recognition rather than torn down with criticism, negativity or put downs. There are far more people in this world that are comfortable putting people down than know how to be positive or positively motivate people. This crew had much fewer problems grasping this concept and was a pretty amazing group.

Deb and I left for Morocco the day before Christmas. We changed planes to a Royal Air Moroc flight at JFK bound for Agadir. We were boarded on the plane and everything was going well. Then it began snowing and they took us off the airplane. They refused to bring me my wheelchair. I sat on the plane till the last possible minute, even breaking down in tears begging them to bring me my own wheelchair, but they would not. They forced me into one of the airport chairs and the worker commented after much protest as I began to comply and surrender, "Now that's a good girl." It was miserable. They kept moving us from terminal to terminal and jerking us around. Everyone was upset and it nearly broke out into a riot many times throughout the ordeal. Eventually they got us on the plane and on our way. We arrived at our final destination; however, my wheelchair did not.

In Morocco while preparing the boat and food I opened my box to find rats had ravaged it and I had lost twenty days of my food supply. I lost forty meals at about $5.00 a pop! Liz Koenig lost about six meals. I was so angry I had to go outside the gate of the boat yard and let out a big yell. What a waste. Deb and I paid a great deal of money to have a space big enough to sort the food at the house but the authorities would not allow us to move food from the boat to the house, so our grand plan was ruined and we incurred extra costs from customs and port authorities. Expedition food is not replaceable in Morocco.

They clearly did not see past our pocketbooks and into the future where ocean rowers can contribute greatly to their economy. It would be better for them in the long run to welcome us and ensure our safety and success of our rowing projects. There are other places in the world to row from. I know I do not want to go back there.

The negative symptoms of life without my own personal wheelchair had become evident with more back, shoulder and wrist pain. The crew tried to help me out as much as possible and did not mind pushing me around nearly as much as I minded. We would leave the boathouse at dark, so avoiding all of the obstacles became more difficult. Abrupt stopping when hitting an obstacle nearly injured the person pushing me and nearly ejected me from the wheelchair numerous times. The wheelchair footplates kept falling off and the wheel fell off once. It was quite risky and dangerous to contend with before the crossing. I am always reminded that most of the time it is far more difficult just getting to the starting line than it is to row across the finish line.

Once the boat was in the water we rowed it around to the marina in Agadir, where we loaded it with our food and personal kit and then waited for the right weather to leave. We got underway the next morning at first light. It wasn't long before one of the members of our crew, Tom Butscher, became violently ill. Food poisoning was suspect. I too had contracted some kind of viral infection, which combined with stress and physical exertion triggered my myasthenia gravis. Myasthenia gravis is an auto immune disease that is ocular, or affects the muscles in the eyes. I have bouts of temporary blindness or double vision. The eyes will cross or eye lids droop or not open at all. The crew may have been concerned about it at first but then saw that I could manage rowing and getting around on the boat without my vision. We had to change our route and head down the coast to Tarfya, Morocco. We then called the Ocean Rowing Society and changed our port of record departure to Tarfya. We had some medical tests done and spoke with a medic there about Tom. He seemed to have recovered enough to continue. My physical condition had improved also and I was managing with medication. When the tide came up at 7:25 p.m. we resumed our row.

Finally underway again at 7:25PM

The northeast wind and weather kept us from going west and we found ourselves going southwest down the coast a bit before the winds changed and we could finally go west. The winds did not favor us on this trip and I almost always found myself rowing against the wind. We had some thirty to thirty-five knot winds and made over 106 miles in one day. If that would have continued we would have had a chance at the record but that was only one day. The rest of the days we averaged about 65-70 miles.

We had a solar water boiler made by the students of an engineering class at Cal State Los Angeles. The instructor Sam Landsberger was a contact I had made at the Abilities Expo in LA. I had tested it at the dock and found it to be working but it had stopped working when we were at sea. We just assumed that it was the wind that prevented it from heating up. Wind was not blowing at the dock. We set it aside and forgot about it till our fuel shortage made it necessary to try and repair the boiler. The intake pump was broken and not sealing so it did not have the suction to move the water and there was a blockage not letting the full amount of water to release from the boiler. I was able to clear the blockage and David fixed the pump for me. After that it worked great. The solar water boiler allowed us to heat water without using the precious little stove fuel we had left. I also built a solar oven out of a dry bag, and an emergency blanket. The solar boiler only makes enough water to rehydrate two meals at a time. This solar oven allowed us to keep the meals warm whilst waiting for the other meals to rehydrate.

Solar water heater on bow of Big Blue

I also experimented with food in the last week as we had run out of regular rations. I made some pizzas from assorted left over bits in the solar oven that were pretty tasty. With the exception of fifty Cliff bars there was not one scrap of food left when we got to port. Everyone had snack packs through the last day. We began rationing regular meals at seven days out, cutting one meal and having breakfast and whatever meal pack happened to be pulled for the day, a lunch or a dinner.

The Sat Phone battery charging port broke on the satellite phone so I also had to fabricate an external battery charger. Debs called Iridium and found out which contacts were positive and which were negative. Then I cut the plug off and David and I put some wire connecters on the ends of the wire. I then used a piece of plastic and a rubber band to keep the connecters against the contact points. Watching all of the episodes of Macgyver as a child paid off!

On the ocean there are amazing moonrises, sunrises and moon- and sunsets. There are panoramic ocean views, and the sky can be brilliantly specked with stars or can be so dark and cloud covered you cannot see your hand in front of your face. Extreme gratitude is what you feel when you get any amount of light to see at night. There is only a certain amount of serenity at night as it is mostly tempered with anxiety as the walls of water crashing down on you are highly anticipated yet invisible in the darkness. There is no way of knowing when, where or how, just that it will repeatedly beat you and knock you off your seat till you change watch. It can feel like the longest two hours of your life.

Being that low in the water not only do you get completely soaked, but you also get pelted by flying fish. There are fish around the boat constantly—dolphins, whales, dorado, tuna, sea turtles, sharks, jelly fish and the occasional Portuguese man of war. We witnessed nature, the food chain or big fish eat little fish many times when the dorado would hunt the flying fish and the shark would then hunt the dorado. Once we even tried catching a wounded dorado that was swimming at the back of our boat to protect it from the shark that had injured it. But we thought better of it, much too risky since the shark was following closely waiting for the kill and the inevitable demise of that beautiful fish.

Big Blue and crew arrive in Port St. Charles, Barbados

When the sky has shades of magenta in it at sunset the reflection in the water looks like liquid silver; when the sky is yellowish the water looks like molten gold. You are like the wind and the water, always moving. Not only does the water change color, but the smell of it changes as well depending on the salinity. There is no smell of land, no pollution, only humidity. Even the water you drink is desalinated ocean water with no chemicals or chlorine in it. When I look out over the ocean and at the GPS and think how privileged I am to be able to be at this place and at this time where no human being has been or may ever be again, I am truly thankful for my life! Then it's back to reality, a piece of plastic trash floats by and I am, once again, disgusted by the human race.

We rowed into port in Port St. Charles Barbados forty-seven days later to our awaiting friends and families. Barbados is amazing and the people there are extremely hospitable and courteous. The specialty at most restaurants is flying fish. I was surprised to find out how tasty they are. Deb went to the Veterans hospital and got a better loaner chair for me to use while there. It was so much better than that crappy airport chair and I was grateful to have it, but I was still missing my personal wheelchair. To this very day that particular wheelchair is still missing.

I changed sports and became a thrower of shot-put and javelin,
returning to the Paralympics in 2012

In spite of a strong competitive desire for a better result in the sport I loved, I left adaptive rowing after Beijing, albeit after numerous attempts to make some needed changes in the leadership of the sport. I so hate the politics involved in sports (and there is plenty in adaptive sports too; don't think we get to escape anything by being disabled or adaptive). I exchanged e-mails with leadership, and copies of emails where I was berated and victimized by people in leadership positions who should have been able to make a difference or change some of the dynamics and behaviors that were occurring to some of the athletes in the sport. I was not singled out and alone; however, I may have been the only one capable of speaking up. And yet, I was alone in that I had no back up and no support. Athletes, including my own double partner, who could have substantiated my claims, was so afraid of never being able to compete for the national adaptive rowing team that he would not speak up. I chose not to file the official complaint which would have led to an investigation requiring all of those in the know about the problems to come forward. I had to believe that a promise of resolution from the leadership would solve the problems and that future athletes would not have to endure such hardship, so I was persuaded not to file an official complaint.

In the meantime, I continued my ocean rowing odyssey and when the schedule permitted I attended the Veterans Wheelchair games just as I had done in the beginning of my road to recovery. I decided to sign up for field events. I received so much positive encouragement from the field coach for the Puerto Rico team I decided to check it out. He said I could be a thrower, so I officially left rowing and switched sports as I could not go back to rowing. The governing body for the sport never removed the problem so it would have been like putting a victimized child back with a battering parent. I learned that villains are everywhere and unfortunately sometimes they are Teflon. I could not take the abuse so I could never go back. The positives are that I could move on to achieve great, GREAT things. Perhaps there had to be a villain to make that happen?

I originally met Cathy Sellers in Beijing and was impressed with her. The next time I saw her was at a Paralympic approved track & field meet in Irvine, California, where I watched other athletes compete from specially designed throwing chairs and I learned more about the sport and what I needed to do to get started. I began throwing at meets and qualified for the Military Standard. I was improving and coming closer to qualifying for the National team standards—but not close enough. So, I did what I know to do and sought out a private coach. Soon I started closing the gap. There were no local programs, coaching or places available to learn and practice, so I created my own opportunities rather than using these negatives as an excuse for failure.

The coach I hired was Aaron Volkoff, who in the beginning knew nothing about Paralympics or adaptive sports but was willing to give it a try. He made the transition easily. I also began going to a chiropractor and a massage therapist. I invested in myself and my goals, and the result was that I made the national team as a thrower for the Para Pan American Games in Guadalajara, Mexico. I won a silver medal in shot put. But they then changed the required distance for qualifications at that meet. I was in our team meeting after the day's activities when it is usually announced which athletes qualify as A or B for the national team. According to the distance required going in I fully expected to make it with my throws. But it turned out I did not because the new distance was farther than the world record for my class and I fell short.

My first thoughts were that the new distance was an unattainable goal for me. I had worked so hard and invested so much, and I was so devastated that I cried all night long. I even approached one of my throwing coaches about quitting. I was reminded by my javelin coach, Erica Wheeler, that I had done an amazing job getting as far as I had in such a short time, and she encouraged me to not give up or quit.

When I got back home I dug in, added more training and worked harder. I had to budget and do without to make it happen because training is expensive. I'd had much experience in doing just that with my ocean rowing campaigns and this was not the first time I allowed myself to believe that something was not achievable for me. I go through what I have to and then I usually attack the goal or mission with a renewed purpose and a vengeance. It wasn't long before I had broken that world record and made the A standard and the Paralympic Team headed for London in 2012. I broke the world record three times leading up to the Paralympics, which was fantastic but did have its downside. Mixed classification events use a point system and the world record is a determining factor in that system. This made it more difficult for my classification of 56 to win against the class 54 and 55's. It took me a long time to understand the point system and that's all I do, understand it. After almost two years in the sport I by no means have it figured out. In London, at the 2012 Paralympics I threw 8.88 meters, which was farther than all sixteen women throwing and two centimeters farther than the one other class 56 that is my competition. It was good for a bronze medal and a Paralympic record, but short of my 9.46 world record. It was not my best performance. My myasthenia gravis was acting up and knowing I would have to throw well over and beyond my world record to win first or or even second in my event, I was psyched out mentally. I also had to contend with the prospect of being confronted by the rowing coach and facing the whistle blowing consequences of lodging legitimate complaints after Beijing. As a lifelong athlete the fondest memories I have were those that were developed from my positive coach-athlete experiences in my high school years. It's one of the reasons I love to participate in sports. It was a far bigger disappointment not to be able to have that in Beijing than it was to lose by such a close margin.

I never discussed any of my anxiety over past Paralympics with Cathy Sellers, my new coaches, the leadership of athletics, the sports physiologist or with the Paralympic committee, so no one knew what I was going through leading up to and in London except for Debs. She came to London and I spent a great deal of my off time away from the venue avoiding confrontation with the demons from my past. I was also able to take some time and go to Ireland, finalizing the deal to purchase my solo ocean rowing boat.

I had an amazing experience in this new sport and I was able to have the coach-athlete experience that was missing in 2008. In an attempt to mitigate my guilt and right the wrong, I made an appointment with the Athlete Ombudsman and shared the complete story and the new athlete complaints. I also gave the athletes the contact information for the ombudsman and encouraged them to lodge their complaints with our representative there. I did all I could do for them.

I had an amazing career in adaptive rowing as an athlete and a promising future at one time as a U.S. Rowing level III coach. I did not necessarily leave all that for ocean rowing, but it did leave me available to pursue more goals in that area that have led to amazing accomplishments and lifetime experiences that could not be matched anyplace on earth.

———

With the Paralympics behind me, it was time to move on to my ocean rowing project. I really wanted to row an ocean solo. The task of rowing across an ocean in any boat with any number of crew is extremely difficult and dangerous.

There was strong opposition for my solo row and encouragement from my friend and coach Cathy Sellers to remain on the national team and to compete in Lyon, France, at the World Championships in 2013, but it was not enough to persuade me. I had chosen 2013 to row because I had my boat, I was physically and mentally ready to go and the Trans Pacific Sailing race would be going on briefly during my row, offering the possibility of occasional VHF radio transmissions and conversations with the sailors participating in the race that will not be available in 2014. The Trans Pacific Sailing Race runs every other year. Completing the row in 2013, or even 2014, would leave me enough time to prepare for the next Paralympic summer games in Rio. After London and my amazing athletic team experience, I took a leave of absence from throwing and resigned from the national team to pursue my other goal: Rowing across the Pacific Ocean solo.

CHAPTER 17:
A SOLO ROW ACROSS THE PACIFIC

My next rowing adventure was to go from from Santa Cruz, California, to Waikiki, Hawaii in a solo rowing boat, dedicating the trip to our military and veterans who have sacrificed so much for our country. My boat, the *Spirit of Orlando*, was named in tribute to my friend Orlando, a fellow ocean rower, adventurer and Royal Marine who was tragically killed in a plane accident on May 15, 2011. He was twenty-six years of age.

Spirit of Orlando

Did I have fears about whether I would be able to make such a journey? You bet! I have fears and doubts every time I set out to row an ocean. I was speaking at an elementary school and one young girl asked, "Do you get scared?" I immediately responded, "No," and I have regretted saying that ever since because it wasn't true. I certainly don't want anyone to think I am afraid of anything but I also don't want people getting the impression that people who accomplish what I have need to be fearless. Fear and doubt are a big part of what motivates me, and it is perfectly normal. It helps drive me to succeed and makes me train and prepare to accomplish what most people consider impossible. I fear failure but am not afraid to do extremely difficult things. I simply train hard and prepare. I'll make a 110% effort for a chance at either succeeding or failing, while being scared shitless the entire time. Most people consider what I do crazy. People have a difficult time grasping the concept of the harshness of life at sea for so much time for anyone let alone a paraplegic with rods in her back. I would be fifty-three years old when I set off on this adventure, and I felt every bit of it.

The Honor the Fallen pre-row paddle

This being my first solo would make it the most difficult physical and mental challenge since my hospitalization and surgeries. Because this row would be taking place in the USA and not half way across the world, organizations such as Shared Adventures; the Northwest Regional Paralympic

Sport Clubs of Sacramento, Santa Cruz, Menlo Park and Monterey; and the VA hospital and others organized the departure as I trained and prepared the boat. I would be rowing solo, but I would have much more land support than I had ever had in my life. I would not be alone on this one; many would be following online. My arrival in Hawaii had the potential to be the most significant celebration in the history of ocean rowing!

It would be redundant to describe the project from inception to start line because it was relatively the same as Rowoflife. All of the drama, all of the ups and downs, all of the same processes and the usual villains, even one that tried to buy the boat out from under me (good effort, Mate).

The row was scheduled to begin at noon on June 8 and a sendoff organized and attended by friends, family and sponsors was planned. We went ahead with the ceremony and launched all kayaks and stand-up paddle boards, and performed an Honor Paddle in the Santa Cruz harbor. The start was delayed till June 9th at 5:45 pm due to weather and high surf caused by a low pressure system, which was on its way out. New weather reports and forecasts looked promising. I made my way out of the Santa Cruz channel at 5:45 pm with only mild onshore NW winds and a relatively flat sea.

Rowing out of Santa Cruz Harbor

I was escorted out to the one-mile buoy by the Harbor Patrol and the Coast Guard, and I saw my first dolphin in the first hour as the sun was setting. The seas and winds remained calm through the night and the sky was clear enough to see many stars. I rowed all through the night making about twenty-six miles and rowed through the morning. The winds had begun to pick up so I put out my parachute anchor at 1:00 pm to take a two hour nap. Sleep did not come in this rest period, partly from me just being so excited and partly because the boat wasn't setting well. I exited the cabin to the sounds of sea lions playing, which was all good until I saw what they were playing with. They had collapsed my para anchor and were playing ball with the buoy I had attached to the rig! They saw me come out of the cabin and stopped, first looking at each other, then at me, and then at each other again like mischievous children. That would completely explain the oddities of the behavior of my boat on sea anchor that first time. I retrieved my para anchor and continued rowing increasing my distance from land and making the most miles west I would see the entire row.

Out on the open sea

As the sun was setting another low pressure system was moving in producing increases in NW winds and in the size of the waves. It was as if the opportunity for good weather to begin my row was like the eye of the storm. I placed my sea anchor out when it became too difficult to row, and thought about the day's events and all of the marine life I had seen in just one day of rowing. It began with the sea lions and a killer whale charging toward my boat, a short time later followed by many dolphins. Then as I was rowing a blue whale and her calf surfaced right beside me. I had to pull in my oar to avoid contact. They left me and headed in closer to shore possibly to avoid the killer whales. Orcas like to go after the whale calves. Not too much later I was charged by more killer whales. My previous encounters with them did not diminish the fear I felt watching them get closer. I had seen two killer whales on the Great Britain row that exhibited the same behavior. They charge toward the boat at rates of speed capable of pulling a water skier, with their huge dorsal fins broaching the surface the entire time. They get just up to the boat threatening to ram you and then disappear. I also saw some interesting looking jellyfish floating by and thought about Diane Nyad, who swims oceans and has nasty encounters with them. And I was visited by three black tip sharks.

Weather system relevant to the *Spirit of Orlando's* position

The NOAA weather channel on the VHF radio described this new low pressure system and small craft and high wind and sea advisories. I set my sleep alarm for two hours so I could check for ship traffic knowing there was little chance I would be rowing again anytime soon. I checked traffic every two hours through the night and as promised the NW winds had reached twenty-five knots with thirty-three to thirty-nine knot gusts. The seas were at about fifteen feet with an additional four to five foot wind swell, so sets topped off about twenty to twenty-five feet. I remained on sea anchor all day and another night. Checking the lines first light I noticed that the anchor bridal lines had chafed and broken and the only line holding my sea anchor on was the one retrieval line I had put it on as an assistive device to help bring the bridal thimble or anchor line attachment point back to the boat. The retrieval line which runs all the way out to the parachute anchor had come undone. I figured that those playful sea lions had broken the bite on my Bolin knot and it had come undone during the night. I had no way to collapse and retrieve my parachute anchor to repair the anchor line fixation points. This was serious as I was about to lose my nine foot diameter parachute anchor, which is an extremely important piece of storm kit.

I also brought a six foot diameter anchor with a much shorter line as a backup. I managed to get about 170 feet of line back in the boat and parachute within fifteen feet of my boat, but could get it no closer. I then took the small anchor and connected it to the rear of my boat deploying it with fifty feet of line. As it opened it swung my boat around to a point where I could reach the other anchor. I had successfully rescued my anchor but sacrificed the smaller less important one as I did not have time to place a retrieval line on it when I deployed it. Pulling a fully laden 1,200 pound boat up to a six foot diameter parachute anchor in twenty-five to thirty mph winds would be easier than the larger diameter para anchor, but I figured I would solve that problem later. The boat was riding fine on the smaller one for the time being. It did get calm enough for me to row again and I figured out how to collapse the chute by sending a carabineer down the anchor line that was bigger than the swivel shackle. It went over the connectors and worked its way down collapsing the chute. Then it came in easy. I had managed to save both anchors, but in the process I had injured my right knee. It locked up and had swollen and would not straighten. It never got calm enough for me to repair the bridal or for me to crawl out onto the bow and make a connection with the bow tow eye located at the front of the boat. My thought was that if I had too, in an emergency, I could use the one located at the rear as I could connect it from my cabin by accessing it through the hatch and that I could make these repairs as well as doing my personal admin and laundry when I got some better conditions at sea.

Bad weather and destroyed anchor bridle

For all of my rowing, in those conditions I could make no west but could only go south. I expected to go a bit south and more southwest and almost do a course that resembled a Nike swoosh, but it was not to be. I had to take the foot stretchers out because of my knee and try to secure myself while rowing with my other leg. I looked at the course and how I could only go southeast in these conditions, took into consideration my knee injury and my distance from land. I was 80.7 miles from land. I decided to row to Los Angeles and reschedule the Hawaii row. I changed my course and rowed southeast. Unfortunately, I did not know about the new forecast at this time.

The seas once again were getting bigger and the winds began howling. I looked at my last two hours of rowing and noticed I had gone more west while rowing southeast. Maybe the current was running west, I thought? Could I possibly make it to Hawaii if I now could somehow go west or had I gone too far south? What was the weather forecast? I turned on the VHF and listened to the forecasts of gale force winds for my location and heavy seas. This basically meant conditions twice as big and bad as what I had been battling for the previous five days were on the menu for the next five days.

There was no question of continuing now, only the realization that I could neither row to Hawaii or Los Angeles in what was coming my way. Staying on the boat, I knew, would jeopardize me or anyone who may have to be involved in a last minute rescue. I called the Coast Guard to apprise them of my situation and ask for their recommendation, and then we co-ordinated rescue from that point forward.

The container ship *MOL Mission* was in my area and dispatched to pick me up. When the ship arrived they determined that they could not dispatch their little boat in the conditions and that they would attempt a direct pick up from the side bay door fifteen feet up on the container ship and that this would occur while the container ship was underway. They instructed me to get up on deck and I was in the process of exiting the cabin when the massive container ship did a drive by along my port side while throwing life rings and lowering a basket. Someone was yelling, "Jump! JUMP!"

But I could not jump and my bum knee, which kept me half in the cabin and not on the deck in time to try to jump, probably saved my life. The sounds of the voices yelling were no longer audible, drowned out by the sounds of my antenna, navigation light and the side and top of my boat scraping along the hull of the huge container vessel as it sucked my little boat beneath its hull at the stern. I gazed up at the hull of the ship atop my little boat and across to the propeller as I got back in my cabin, closing the hatch door to ride out what was coming next.

The huge container ship sucked me up and spit me out the back in a haze of propeller wash. Foamy and turbulent, the water glowed a sea foam green that seemed to give off its own amazing light. Then darkness settled and with no daylight left the giant spotlights on the ship were turned on, panning the dark sea looking for me. They then contacted me on the radio about making another pass.

After being at sea for seven days and battling bad weather for the last five as I stayed out on the deck waiting, hanging on, getting slammed by fifty-four degree water waves in fifty-five degree outside temps, I thought about what I had just gone through. I hailed the ship on the radio and waved him off of any further rescue attempts. Anyone in my position would not have been physically capable of what was required. The ship's captain wanted to rescue me as much as I wanted to row to Hawaii, so he was not happy to leave me in my little boat. But I thought it best and I stuck to my guns. I thanked him for his time and effort and told both he and the Coast Guard that I was going to warm up, go to sleep and further assess my situation in the morning. I was going to sleep on it.

At about 2:45 am the Coast Guard called me and told me they would have a helicopter to my location in about an hour. They arrived and a rescue swimmer was deployed. I made sure to leave the navigation light on the *Spirit of Orlando* to aide in recovery of the boat. The swimmer got back in the water first, then I joined him. He swam us over to the basket, placed me in it and I was raised up into the helicopter. It was a text book sea rescue. I phoned Deb and told her I would be at the Santa Barbara Airport where she met me with some dry clothes and my wheelchair. We spent the rest of the day on the drive back stopping at vessel assist in Ventura, who told us it would be impossible to go out and get the boat in the weather that was coming and that there was no way to know where to look anyway. We stopped at military installations and ports and harbors asking them to look out and contact us if they spotted the boat.

I was at sea from 5:45 pm on June 9 until 3:45 am on June 17 when *Spirit of Orlando* was left adrift. I rowed a total of 172 miles.

Map of the *Spirit of Orlando's* journey

THE SEARCH FOR *SPIRIT OF ORLANDO*

The search for the boat began as soon as I made landfall on June 17, 2013. Deb and I stopped every place between Santa Barbara (the point of extraction eighty miles west of Morro Bay) and Long Beach, sharing pictures of the boat and speaking with people. We wondered how far a small boat with a parachute or drag anchor deployed would drift before making landfall. When I was on the boat it was only drifting six to nine miles a day in a southeasterly direction whilst on sea anchor; however, that was not in strong winds.

It had been three weeks since my rescue and we hadn't had any news. We decided to be more proactive and booked a Channel Islands whale watching tour with Island Packers to go out looking for my little boat on a Sunday. Once there we gave out more *Spirit of Orlando* picture cards and talked to more people. We had a fun day but had no success finding my boat. We took the coastal drive home and I kept a lookout using a pair of binoculars just hoping for a sighting. We were nearly home when we received a Facebook message from Denise Muller that stated the boat had been found in San Diego. I was opening my computer to go online and look at the message when I got a call from Catherine Miller informing me that a long range fishing boat named *Old Glory* had found my ocean rowing boat. She said that they were towing it in and that it would arrive at 6:00 am Monday morning. We quickly called the Navy Lodge and booked a room for Sunday night. We then hooked up the trailer and were on our way to San Diego so that we could be there when the boat arrived in the morning.

We did not know what to expect as that was a considerable distance, hundreds of miles farther than expected. We got to San Diego at 1:00 am and managed to get three hours of sleep before heading to the H&M Landing at 5:20 in the morning. All kinds of thoughts ran wildly through my mind. What condition would the boat be in? Would I have enough money to pay for my boat's recovery? According to salvage laws they did not have to give me my boat and could ask whatever price they wanted for it. What if I did not have enough? I have Search and Recovery Insurance for myself and Vessel Assist for recovery of the boat up to 100 miles, but It has to be recovered by a specific Vessel Assist boat. It was looking as though I would have to cover the costs myself.

The *Spirit of Orlando* (foreground) alongside Old Glory

When we arrived at the marina there was an ABC 10 news van there and a lot of people getting ready to go out fishing. It was sunrise and daylight began penetrating the marine layer. Our eyes searcjed the H&M Landing for the boat. First we followed the news crew power cord to the back of the building by the gangway that lead to the dock with all of the commercial fishing boats where the news reporter was busy shooting a piece; we went past them down the gangway. The tide was out and the ramp steep so I positioned myself at the top, lifted both front wheels up and proceeded to ride a wheelie all the way down the ramp. My backpack was hitting the anti-slip surface making a dragging noise that got the attention of the reporter and the cameraman. I turned to see where Deb was and was blinded by the light on the camera. I wondered if I should have approached them but I was in a hurry to get to the boat.

Old Glory was almost to the end of the boat dock and was unloading the fishermen who were aboard for *Spirit of Orlando's* recovery. Just down to the right on the dock before *Old Glory* I spotted my little boat. I had not seen all of the damage done in the container ship incident as it happened at night and I was extracted from the boat in the cover of darkness. Other than a broken antenna, navigation light and flag staff she looked to be in pretty good shape. There were some scrapes in the 3M wrap but they didn't seem to even go down to the gel coat.

It was a very emotional reunion and I got teary eyed remembering how close a call that really was—and how much worse it could have been. The reporter and cameraman made it down to the boat. I felt a little embarrassed being teary eyed and getting caught on camera. I suppressed my tears and then did a brief interview with Channel 10. I was distracted during the interview by my own anxiousness to get aboard *Spirit of Orlando,* and as soon we were finished I transferred onto the boat and opened the cabin door. It was a little damp and the contents were all topsy-turvy like the boat had possibly pitched poled (going bow over stern); it definitely had rolled over and self-righted at least once. The airlines' statement "contents shift during flight" came to mind.

Deb told me the boat owner was ready to talk to me so I transferred back over to my chair and went to meet the owner and skipper of *Old Glory*. They helped me aboardtheir ship and I sat inside the galley waiting anxiously as it was time to discuss business. I was so afraid I would not have enough money. Joe Philips, the owner/operator of *Old Glory* told me how he supports veterans and how they take our wounded warriors out fishing. Then he told me he was not going to charge me. I offered money to cover expenses and fuel but he and the crew refused to take any money. I was relieved and put off at the same time as I wanted to give them something. All I can do for now is express my gratitude. They were all so generous and kind. The skipper had looked up information about my boat and the tribute row, and it is my understanding that all consented unanimously to the recovery of the *Spirit of Orlando* without charge.

———————

I have created a Facebook page (Military & Veteran Tribute Row) and the website *http://www.rowoflife.com*, where people can follow my adventures online and where pictures, video and blogs of past and present projects can be viewed. Upon completion of a solo row I will be one of the most accomplished female ocean rowers on the planet having completed four ocean crossings and a circumnavigation of Great Britain, and will be the only disabled woman to have rowed an ocean solo or single handed. I can already say that I am the *only* paraplegic or disabled woman on the planet who rows across oceans.

As I am currently recovering from one knee surgery while awaiting surgery on the other, I can't say if I will have a speedy and full enough recovery in time to make another go at it before the 2016 Paralympics where I look forward to continuing my rivalry with the German thrower and breaking and setting some more records. There is a great amount of uncertainty for me not knowing if my body will recover enough for me to realistically make another solo rowing attempt. The surgeon did not have a very positive opinion; but when has that ever stopped me before? I am, after all, a paraplegic that rows across oceans. I can't tell you how many times I have been told I would not be able to do so and yet I have proved them all wrong every time. That is something that I reserve and deserve the right to decide for myself. The *Spirit of Orlando* waits for me in a storage facility while I recover physically and psychologically from the beating I received on my fist failed attempt to row solo across the Pacific Ocean. I remain on standby to try again as quitting and giving up are not my style.

I don't know what the future holds for me or how many more sunsets I will chase, rowing across oceans and against the wind.

EPILOGUE

From 1981 to 1996 I was angry and always questioning, "Why me?" It was easy to give up and give in to despair. The only things I could count were my losses, not my blessings. At the time, the losses were so much greater and I never could see that what had happened to me could actually be a blessing until I began moving on with my new and different life. However, it wasn't easy to move on into such an uncertain future. I was not seeing hope for anything positive and meaningful, just anticipating a life of pain and suffering. When I began participating in sports again, it was familiar. It was different, yet the same; a vehicle to restore me, to restore my hope, and to arouse my competitive spirit. I have never looked back or ever felt as completely hopeless as I did back then. I cannot imagine ever feeling like that again. I know what it is to suffer. I know what it is to feel hopeless. I know what it feels like to give up on dreams and goals. And I also know what a mistake it is to give up.

There is still great pain and suffering in my life every day through aging and degeneration, my physical condition is sure to deteriorate. Sooner than I would like, I am sure to require another surgery and the thought of being dependent on others and being at their mercy, not being as mobile or independent, being less able to participate in sports as I do now or not being able to participate at all, absolutely terrifies me. I do know that I have many more blessings now to count than I will ever suffer losses. I have had and continue to have the most fantastic life.

172

R E S O U R C E S

rowoflife.com
My official website features pictures, blogs, details about past and upcoming rowing events and important links.

California Adaptive Rowing Programs (CARP)
My non-profit organization provides instruction and training for competitive and recreational opportunities in the sport of rowing for physically and intellectually challenged individuals.
California Adaptive Rowing Programs
3350 E 7th St. #231
Long Beach, CA 90804
Office: (562) 434-8334 Cell:
(562) 505-4157
www.carplb.net

American Wheelchair Table Tennis Association
www.ncpad.org/competitive/fact_sheet.php?sheet=74&section=546
1-800-900-8086
ncpad@uic.edu

Air Force Aid Society
For over sixty-eight years, the Air Force Aid Society has offered worldwide emergency assistance, sponsored education assistance programs and offered an array of base community enhancement programs that improve quality of life for Airmen and their families.
www.afas.org

Armed Services YMCA of the USA

ASYMCA is entirely self-funded through individual donations, corporate contributions and a standing YMCA endowment that pays for military programs and services in full. Except for contracts for services, ASYMCA receives no funding from the U.S. government.

Armed Services YMCA of the USA

National Headquarters

6359 Walker Lane, Suite 200

Alexandria, VA 22310

www.asymca.org

Paralyzed Veterans Association California Chapter

Since 1946 PVA has provided and developed a unique expertise on a wide variety of issues involving the special needs of its members – veterans of the armed forces who have experienced spinal cord injury or dysfunction.

Paralyzed Veterans Association California Chapter

5901 E 7th Street

Bldg 150, Rm. R-204

Long Beach, CA 90822

(562) 826-5713

fax: (562) 494-5140

(800) 497-0565

calpva.org

Disabled Dealer Magazine

A great source for buying or selling accessible vans, motor homes, scooters, wheelchairs, RV's and more.

Disabled Dealer Corporate Office

426 Island Cay Way

Apollo Beach, FL 33572

888-521-8778

www.disableddealer.com

Directory of Sports Organizations for Athletes with Disabilities
www.aapmr.org/condtreat/athletes3.htm

Disabled Sports USA
The mission of Disabled Sports USA is to provide national leadership and opportunities for individuals with disabilities to develop independence, confidence, and fitness through participation in community sports, recreation and educational programs.
www.dsusa.org

Handicapped Scuba Association
Founded in 1981, and made up of over 4,000 underwater educators, scuba divers with disabilities and supporting members, is located in over forty-five countries. The handicapped scuba association is dedicated to assuring that people with disabilities are given the same opportunity to receive quality-training, certification and dive adventures as the able bodied population.
www.hsascuba.com

National Wheelchair Basketball Association
The National Wheelchair Basketball Association (NWBA) is comprised of **over 200** basketball teams across twenty-two conferences and seven divisions, and provides qualified individuals with physical disabilities the opportunity to play, learn and compete in the sport of wheelchair basketball.
National Wheelchair Basketball Association
1130 Elkton St., Suite C
Colorado Springs, Colorado 80907
(719) 266-4082
Fax: (719) 266-4876
E-Mail: toddhatfield@nwba.org—Executive Director
www.nwba.org

U.S. Handcycling Association

The United States Handcycling Federation is a non-profit corporation designed to create integrated cycling opportunities for wheelchair users and athletes with lower-mobility impairments.

(831) 457-7747

www.ushf.org

U.S. Paralympics

U.S. Paralympics, a division of the U.S. Olympic Committee is dedicated to becoming the world leader in the Paralympic sports movement and promotes excellence in the lives of people with physical disabilities. Since its formation in 2001, the U.S. Paralympics has been inspiring Americans to achieve their dreams through education, sports programs and partnerships with community organizations, medical facilities and government agencies.

United States Olympic Committee

U.S. Paralympics Division

One Olympic Plaza

Colorado Springs, CO 80909

719-866-2030

(Fax) 719-866-2029

www.usparalympics.org

U.S. Quad Rugby Association

The United States Quad Rugby Association provides opportunity, support, and structure for competitive wheelchair rugby to people with disabilities.

James T. Gumbert, USQRA Commissioner

11104 Spicewood Club Drive

Austin, Texas 78750

(512) 791 2644

www.quadrugby.com

U.S. Wheelchair Weightlifting Federation
39 Michael Place
Levittown, PA 19057
(215) 945-1964

Wheelchair & Ambulatory Sports USA
WSUSA is a non-profit and member of the U.S. Olympic Committee and provides guidance and support to local clubs and community-based organizations as well as conduct regional competitions which allows athletes to qualify for national events and international teams.
Wheelchair & Ambulatory Sports USA
1236 Jungerman Rd., Suite A
St. Peters, MO 63376
636-614-6784
www.wsusa.org

World Association for Persons With Disabilities
WAPD advances the interests of persons with disabilities at national, state, local and home levels.
www.wapd.org

Youth For Human Rights
A non-profit whose aim is to teach youth about human rights, and inspire them to become advocates for tolerance and peace.
Youth For Human Rights
1954 Hillhurst Ave. #416
Los Angeles, CA 90027
(323) 663-5799
www.youthforhumanrights.org

Wheelchair Sports, USA

Founded in 1956 as the National Wheelchair Athletic Association, Wheelchair Sports, USA is dedicated to promoting sports for adults and youths with physical disabilities.

Wheelchair Sports, USA
10 Lake Circle Suite G19
Colorado Springs, CO 80906
(719) 574-1150
www.apparelyzed.com/support/sport/wsusa.html

WHEELCHAIR SPORTS, USA: REGIONAL SPORTS ORGANIZATIONS

Appalachian Wheelchair Athletic Association
22 Mitchell Drive
Abingdon, MD 21009
(410) 669-7215
fax: (410) 669-7215
gherman@abs.net

Dixie Wheelchair Athletic Association
3230 Skyland Drive SW
Snellville, GA 30078
(770) 978-8183

Far West Wheelchair Athletic Association
Gerard Manuel
5730 Chambertin Drive
San Jose, CA 95118
(408) 978-2828
or (408) 267-0200
fax: 408-267-2834

Long Island Wheelchair Athletic Club
Wheelchair Basketball
Long Island Express
P. O. Box 718
Holbrook, New York 11741
(631) 689-9729
http://home.interserv.com/~bobsel
BLIWAC@Mindspring.com

Michigan Wheelchair Athletic Association
144 10 Vale Court
Sterling Heights, MI 48312
(810) 446-2489
fax: (810) 977-6239

Mid-Atlantic Wheelchair Athletic Association
Box 103, WWRC
Fishersville, VA 22939
332-7184
fax: (540) 332-7394

New England Wheelchair Athletic Association
MA Hospital School
3 Randolph Street
Canton, MA 02021
(781) 828-2440 ext.388

North Central Wheelchair Athletic Association
Courage Center
3915 Golden Valley Road
Golden Valley, MN 55422
(612) 520-0479
fax: (612) 520-0577

Northwest Wheelchair Sports Association
PO Box 1596
Big Timber, MT 59011
(406) 932-5237

Rocky Mountain Wheelchair Athletic Association
1080 South Independence Court
Lakewood, CO 80226
(303) 982-4211
mcarpent@jeffco.k12.co.us

Southeastern Wheelchair Athletic Association
Rt. 25 Box 346
Fayetteville, NC 28306
(910) 323-9010 ext. 334

Southwest Wheelchair Athletic Association
705 West Avenue B #300
Garland, TX 75040
(972) 494-3160

Tri-State Wheelchair Athletic Association
157-23 20th Road
Whitestone, NY 11357
(718) 767-6677

Wheelchair Sports, Hawaii
95-1086 Lalai Street
Honolulu, HI 96789
(808) 943-1250

U.S. Electric Wheelchair Hockey Association

Power Hockey
7216 39th Avenue North
Minneapolis, MN 55427
(763) 535-4736
CraigM@PowerHockey.com
link: www.PowerHockey.com

Wheelchair Archers, USA
528 N. Bauman Street
Indianapolis, IN 46214
(317) 244-2377

Wheelchair Athletics of the USA
2351 Parkwood Road
Snellville, GA 30278
(770) 972-0763
fax: (770) 985-4885
bewing@bellsouth.net

National Wheelchair Basketball Association
1100 Blythe Blvd.
Charlotte, NC 28203
(704) 355-1064
fax: (704) 446-4999
nwba@carolinas.org

Wheelchair Fencing
4009 Woodgate Lane
Louisville, KY 40220
(502) 582-5734
marcella.m.denton.@usace.army.mil

Handcycling Federation
115 Du Four St.
Santa Cruz, CA 95060
(831) 457-7747

U.S. Quad Rugby Association
3340 S E Morrison, Apt 380
Portland, OR 97214
(503) 238-1324
ESUHR@aol.com

National Wheelchair Shooting Federation
NRA Disabled Shooting Services
11250 Wales Mill Road
Fairfax, VA 22030
(703) 267-1495
fax: (703) 267-3941

American Sled Hockey Association
21 Summerwood Court
Buffalo, NY 14223
(716) 874-8411 ext. 7327
fax: (716) 874-8518

U.S. Wheelchair Swimming
5730 Chambertin Drive
San Jose, CA 95118
(408) 267-0200
fax: (408) 267-2834

American Wheelchair Table Tennis Association
23 Parker Street
Port Chester, NY 10573
(914) 937-3932

U.S. Wheelchair Weightlifting Federation
39 Michael Place
Levittown, PA 19057
215-945-1964
fax: 215-946-2574

American Amateur Racquetball Association-Wheelchair
Luke St. Onge, Executive Director
1685 West Uintah
Colorado Springs, CO 80904
635-5396
fax: (719) 635-0685

American Disabled Water Skiers
William Furbish
3480 Statfield Drive
Atlanta, GA 30319
(404) 261-9527
fax: (404) 364-9405
bfurbish@mindspring.com

ABOUT THE AUTHOR

Debra and Angela on their wedding day

In September of 1993, at the age of thirty-three, Angela Madsen underwent back surgery for an injury she sustained while on duty in the military. Her goal was to be walking and surfing within one year but the surgery went very badly and many mistakes were made, leaving her with an unrepairable spinal cord. But Angela is not defined by the word "disabled."

Angela is a mother of one, grandmother of three, from Long Beach, California, who loves to surf. She is a veteran of the United States Marine Corps and a life member of both the Disabled American Veterans and the Paralyzed Veterans of America. Angela also enjoys working with newly injured vets to get them involved with adaptive sports. In February of 2003, the Amateur Athletic Foundation named Angela as a recipient of the Women Who Inspire Us Award; in September of 2003, she received the Leo Reilly, Jr. Award for outstanding spirit and determination, and also received the 2011 California Paralyzed Veterans Association Legacy of Hope American Spirit Award.

On February 7, 2007, she became the first paraplegic woman to row across the Atlantic Ocean. Her rowing partner, Franck Festor, an amputee from France, did not speak English and Angela does not speak French. They rowed nearly 3,000 miles in sixty-six days, coming in eighth place in the pair's class. There were twenty-two boats in the race and they were the only physically challenged athletes.

Angela competed on the U.S. Rowing Team from 1999 thru 2008 and competed in the 2008 Paralympics in Beijing, China. She is a four-time World Championship Gold Medalist and a Level 3 Rowing Coach. She is the Founder, Director and Coach/Instructor of the California Adaptive Rowing Program (www.carplb.net) a non-profit program founded in 2000 that teaches disabled people to row. She also assists in the start up of new adaptive rowing programs nationwide.

In 2009, Angela rowed across the Indian Ocean from Geraldton, West Australia, 3,600 miles to Mauritius, an island east of Madagascar, with a crew of eight on a fifty-eight day adventure that set many world rowing records, including the fastest rowing crossing of the Indian Ocean. She is now one of the first women and the first and only person with a disability to row across the Indian Ocean, as well as the first disabled woman to row across two oceans.

In 2010, Angela was part of another world record setting rowing crew of four women. They became the first and fastest women's crew to circumnavigate Great Britain, and Angela has become the first and only person with a disability to have rowed the 2,010 miles non-stop and unsupported from London's Tower Bridge, around Great Britain and back to the Tower Bridge in fifty-one days.

In 2011, it was back to the Atlantic, only this time as skipper of a crew of sixteen on a boat called *Big Blue*, he first ocean rowing catamaran. Angela and her crew rowed from Tarfya, Morocco to Barbados in just forty-seven days.

In 2012 Angela set a Paralympic record and won a Bronze medal in the women's class 56 shot-put in London.

Future ambitions and plan include a second attempt at a record-setting 2,500 mile solo rowing crossing of the Pacific Ocean from California to Hawaii and the an appearance at the 2016 Paralympics in Rio de Janeiro.

Angela lives with her wife, Debra Moeller, in Long Beach, California and Bakersfield, California.

―――――